W9-BZN-259

the
exotic fruit
and vegetable
handbook

Oona van den Berg

Project Editor: Sarah Ford
Copy Editor: Joanna Smith
Proof-readers: Clare Hacking and Anne Crane

Creative Director: Keith Martin
Executive Art Editor: Geoff Fennell
Freelance Designer: Justine Harrison

Production Controller: Lisa Moore
Indexer: Hilary Bird

Photographer: Ian Wallace
Home Economist: Oona van den Berg
Stylist: Antonia Gaunt

The Exotic Fruit and Vegetable Handbook by Oona van den Berg

First published in 2000 by Hamlyn
an imprint of Octopus Publishing Group Limited
2–4 Heron Quays, London E14 4JP

Copyright © 2000 Octopus Publishing Group Limited

British Library Cataloguing-in-Publication Data
A catalogue record for this book is available from the British Library

ISBN 0 600 60055 6

Produced by Toppan
Printed in China

Notes

Standard level spoon measurements are used in all recipes.
1 tablespoon = one 15 ml spoon
1 teaspoon = one 5 ml spoon

Both metric and imperial measurements have been given in all recipes. Use one set of measurements only and not a mixture of both.

Eggs should be medium unless otherwise stated.

Do not re-freeze a dish that has been frozen previously.

Ovens should be preheated to the specified temperature – if using a fan assisted oven, follow the manufacturer's instructions for adjusting the time and temperature.

contents

introduction

Colourful, earthy and exhilarating – exotic fruits and vegetables brighten a greengrocer's selection and add a tropical dimension. From the cheeky pink lychee, orange egg-like grenadilla or cerise-pink dragon fruit, to the blue/mauve Congo potato, the greengrocer's display is a rich, exotic, tossed salad or melting pot of ethnic influences. Exotic fruits and vegetables provide a riot of colour and a tantalizing mix of aromas and flavours. They have fast become readily available, as Asian stores and farmers' markets spring up around cities, and crate loads of fresh ingredients are flown in from the market gardens of Kenya, Israel, South America and California. The produce is picked and hits our stores and larger supermarkets within hours. The West Indian, Asian and South American overseas communities have brought with them their own styles of life, cooking and a wonderful selection of ingredients. Their street markets are bursting with colour and are interesting places to shop; scoops of plantains or bundles of

above: Figs

freshly cooked bamboo jostle for position alongside the Brussels sprout and the common potato. This is what is so exciting about food today – the marriage between everyday Western ingredients and exotica. We are living a truly global existence. Foreign travel, magazines and television have brought the other side of the world to our everyday lives and, with all the ingredients now obtainable, this has created a tropical and exotic shopping basket.

Asian, and more recently Latino, cooking have become the buzzwords and trends in restaurants and on their menus. Fusion cooking, the marriage between East and West, is at the forefront of food news. And it is nowhere better executed than in Australia. There the local Asian communities have created a culture of food that Europe has turned to watch, and in doing so, has created some of the most exciting styles of cooking. Pan-Pacific has come of age. It is the cooking of the moment and has created an impact that is likely to stay the course, as food and cooking move closer on a global scale.

above: Drumsticks

Good cooking means an intuitive way with fresh ingredients – taking an ingredient and marrying it to one's own repertoire. We have acquired and learnt so much from the Far East, the Americas and Latin influences, and gleaned and enjoyed the powerful flavours and colours of the produce of these countries. This is no more aptly seen than in the exciting developments happening in the world of sushi, there is no longer just the traditional Japanese version, but sushi that includes carpaccio of beef with a lemon grass pesto, for example. Add to that the vegetables of the East and the wonderful, equally powerful and assertive fruits of South America, and the result adds a dynamic edge to shopping and cooking. Now cooking need never be bland or mundane with the exotic selection currently available at conventional stores or via the Internet. Today our daily shopping is very much part of global trade and is exciting, colourful, dramatic – and fun. Once you know where to go to discover exotic ingredients, you have a chance to develop a relationship with shopkeepers and trade in recipes as well as produce, and shopping elevates itself from an errand to a wonderful pastime.

Asia, Africa and South America are the pivotal points on the culinary map for their cooking styles and, of course, for their fruits and vegetables. The trade in these ingredients began a long time ago. The potato, a treasure of the Andes, was introduced to Europe from South America in the 16th century, while Marco Polo was the first Westerner to taste the nashi pear, in China. During those times ingredients were exchanged for other valuable wares and brought to Europe as botanical samples. These old and ancient exotica are now ingredients that are sent worldwide and are available for all to try and decide on how best to use them. Their other great advantage is that many are available during our lean winter months when the root vegetables and cabbages of Europe are enlivened by the dramatic entrance of the grenadilla, rambutan and other bright and cheery

above: Rambutan

tropical fruits and vegetables.

A great deal of history can be traced back to Europe's discovery of everyday ingredients such as the tomato from South America, garlic from Egypt and Britain's greatest selling fruit, the banana – originally from Asia and now a commercial crop across the subtropics. The great explorers circumnavigated the world and went out in search of the new and the unusual on the way. The Victorians, often thought of as dour serious people, provided some of our greatest adventurers, who travelled far and wide in search of new plants both for their edible and eye-catching characteristics. Without those adventurous spirits the local markets would be far less exciting places and cooking would be a culinary void without the tomato, potato and onion. The cargo ships that crossed the world returned to their home ports loaded with edible ingredients, from spices to fruits and vegetables, for a population who often didn't venture further than the next town. To them the Jerusalem artichoke or aubergine could easily have come from the moon.

So many of these fruits and vegetables are now so widely available because of the advent of worldwide trade. Local Asian, Middle Eastern, Turkish and Cypriot shop owners often have their own sources and family contacts through which they import their own specialities. These stores are well worth investigating for their supplies. Often the best citrus fruits, complete with leaves, can be sourced in a corner shop in one of the communities of Brick Lane, Brixton, Southall or Tooting. Getting to know your local shopkeeper can be well worth it – they'll let you know when the season is or when they have a box going for a song. That's the day you make chutney, sorbet or an aromatic fruit salad of pomelo. That is the way to cook – making use of the best available on that day.

Some of these fruits and vegetables are expensive because of the distance they have travelled and are at their best simply cooked or prepared or, in the case of many fruits, eaten raw and in their prime, to chop or crush them would be a crying shame. To scoop into a fresh mangosteen and enjoy its distinctive sweetness and heights of flavour is far more rewarding than to toss it together in a fruit salad and lose its many nuances. However, there are occasions when the market, supermarket or store will have a glut on their hands and reduce the prices – then it's time to pounce and create a dramatic, memorable dish.

Exporting local produce supports vast communities in Colombia, Chile, Argentina, Africa and California. These communities run on the strength of their trade in local fruits and vegetables. They grow, nurture, harvest and sell the produce and even support spin-off trades, for example in Indian coconut plantations, they also produce copra for matting, garden fertilizers and rope. There the coconut provides a delicious drink, a cooking ingredient and also the tough husk with which to create copra with its many uses. International trade is a tricky and complex business, upset all too easily. If the strength of trade is bad, for example in the South African apple industry, the apple and pear orchards, and the local communities that rely on them, suffer. Another example was the misguided marketing of the kiwi fruit back in the 1970s. It left many a New Zealand farmer without a market and a glut of kiwis that wouldn't shift. The price of the fruit fell to a level that made growing and exporting the fruit unprofitable.

Cooking exotic fruits and vegetables brings an international flavour to the kitchen – the cooking of the Deep South, plantain cakes from the Windward Islands, the coconut curries of the East and the chillies of South America. Our tables and kitchens are becoming global, and experimenting with new or unusual ingredients adds spice to our life and interest to the menu. That's what is exciting about cooking – it's a living, developing art. Like all cultures and ways of life, cooking is constantly evolving and to be apace of it makes a good and interesting cook. It's the understanding of places and people and the ability to transport those flavours home to family and friends as they gather round the table – that's the greatest gift of all.

Support the growers, explore and experiment with exotic ingredients and keep the world spinning on an exchange of exotic produce.

Oona van den Berg

above: Okra

fruit & vegetable directory

fruits 12–49

vegetables 50–81

Actinidia chinensis
Kiwi

The kiwi is the size of a large plum and has an inedible brown furry exterior. It originated in the Yangtze valley in China but is now grown in New Zealand, Australia, South America, France and Italy. Peel off its coat to reveal the bright lime-green flesh, flecked with seeds. It is strange to think that only a few years ago this wonderful fruit was relatively unknown in the West. Now it is popular with children and adults alike for its sweet flesh and high levels of vitamin C.

The name comes from New Zealand where the fruit was first popularized and named after the country's national emblem – the flightless kiwi bird. It is also known, however, as the Chinese gooseberry after its country of origin. It has almost twice as much vitamin C as an orange and a single fruit provides the full daily requirement of vitamin C for an adult. It also supplies potassium, fibre and vitamin E. It contains about 10 per cent sugar and provides about 30 calories per fruit.

To find a ripe kiwi, look for a slightly soft and plump fruit. Ripe kiwis yield when gently pressed. To ripen, leave at room temperature but do not leave close to other fruit since an enzyme in the kiwi causes other fruit to ripen very quickly. The ripe flesh will be soft, juicy and sweet, but with a surprising amount of acidity. The best way to eat a kiwi is like a boiled egg; simply slice off the top and scoop out the flesh with a spoon. They are also great peeled, sliced into rounds and used in fruit salads or as a garnish, as the flesh doesn't discolour.

The flesh of the kiwi is also a good tenderizer for meat. Leave chicken, pork or beef in a kiwi marinade for just 20 minutes before grilling – it makes quite a difference. This enzyme action will also make milk curdle and stop gelatine from setting, so do not be tempted to put kiwi in a jelly. Look out for the golden kiwi – the new kid on the shelf. It is sweet with golden flesh.

recipe using kiwis, see page: 142

Ananas comosus
Queen pineapple

Pineapples are among the most popular of exotic fruits, although once upon a time they were only enjoyed by the very wealthy. Christopher Columbus is thought to have discovered them on the island of Guadeloupe in the 1490s but today these sweet, acidic fruits are readily available to all. They are grown in many tropical countries from Africa to Central America, Hawai to Asia. An average pineapple weighs in at about 1 kg (2 lb), but you can also now buy tiny pineapples, no bigger than a hand, called queen pineapples. These are particularly sweet.

When choosing a ripe pineapple, there should be a strong pineapple aroma, the leaves should be stiff and fresh, and a central leaf should come away easily when gently tugged. The rough skin should glow with a warm orange-gold colour. Inside the flesh is sweet, with quite a lot of acidity, and is deliciously fragrant.

If you cannot find queen pineapples, use a sweet variety of the large pineapple. A new variety called Supersweet is, as its name suggests, packed with sweetness and very little acidity. These pineapples characteristically have a green-gold skin, which would suggest they were not ripe. But this is not the case.

The easiest way to serve a pineapple is to cut it into slices. Remove the outer rind, cut out the little brown eyes with the tip of a sharp knife, then remove the central, fibrous core. A perfectly ripe pineapple needs little else, but it goes well with pork, cheese and spicy fish curries. Pineapple is a good source of vitamin C and recent research has shown that pineapples contain an important enzyme called bromelain that aids digestion by breaking down protein. It is also thought to help sufferers of heart disease as it inhibits blood clotting.

recipes using queen pineapples, see pages: 131; 156

Annona cherimola
Custard apple

Custard apples or chermoyas, as they are also known, are natives of South America and the West Indies and can be seen growing on large shrubs on the slopes of the Andes. These heart-shaped fruits, with their unusual skin that resembles scales, are rather ugly. When pale green they are unripe and at this stage are very hard and almost impossible to cut in half. As they ripen the skin develops brown patches that make the fruit look over-ripe, but in fact it is at just the right point. The creamy white flesh is juicy and has a flavour reminiscent of pineapples and bananas with a delicious vanilla overtone. There are plenty of large black seeds in the soft flesh, up to 20 seeds in one fruit.

Custard apples are difficult to transport when ripe since they squash and bruise easily, so it is best to buy them while still green and ripen them in a paper bag in a warm room. Once ripe, the skin will develop the distinctive brown patches and the flesh should give a little when pressed. At this stage they will keep in the bottom of the refrigerator for a day or two.

To eat, cut in half, scoop out the flesh and discard the skin and seeds. Blend the flesh with bananas and cream for a quick dessert or with water or mango juice for a refreshing drink. This is a nutritious fruit high in vitamin C, niacin, thiamin and iron. Make the most of them when they are available from July to April.

recipe using custard apples, see page. 160

Averrhoea carambola
Carambola

The carambola is a native of South-east Asia and is most often found in Malaysia and Indonesia where it is known as *bilimbi*. It grows on what is often referred to as the 'cucumber fruit tree' which is happiest growing where there is plentiful water. Carambolas can be found growing commercially in Africa, South America and the USA.

When ripe, the fruit turns from green to yellow and when cut the slices are an attractive star shape, which is why it is more often referred to as the star fruit. It has a waxy skin, which can be eaten, and a watery flesh with the occasional pip. It is most often eaten raw in fruit salads or used to decorate puddings and cakes, but when under-ripe and green it is used in the Phillipines for its sour flesh. The green star fruit is roughly chopped and added to sour soups of fish or chicken. The Phillipinos and Malaysians rather enjoy the slightly acidic flavour and also squeeze the fruit to make a refreshing juice. The acidic juice also has medicinal advantages; it is considered good for digestion and is rich in vitamin C and contains some potassium, niacin and phosphorus.

Star fruit can also be made into a spiced chutney to serve with roasted meat or can be gently poached in a sweet lime syrup and served with ice cream.

The difficult thing to judge with star fruit is the best ones to buy – some are sweeter and more flavoursome, but there is no way of knowing which are the best. Select a star fruit with firm, undamaged skin; if it is yellow and slightly soft when you buy it, keep it in the refrigerator until you are ready to use it.

recipe using carambolas, see page: 90

Borrasus flabellifer
Palm fruit

Palm fruits are harvested from the palmyra or toddy palm which grows wild in southern India, Sri Lanka and Burma and is now cultivated throughout South-east Asia. This same palm tree is also tapped to obtain palm wine or toddy, as it is often called, which is drunk by the local people across India and South-east Asia. Each day a toddy tapper climbs the tree and collects the juice that has dripped into a bamboo container fixed under the flower and fermented in the heat of the sun. It is very sweet and an acquired taste.

The shiny nut from this palm contains oval gelatinous seeds that are opaque and very sweet. These seeds are extracted from the hard nut. They have a mild nutty flavour that has gentle coconut tones. In Thailand, Malaysia and Indonesia, palm fruit seeds are used for their sweet and interesting texture and are added to their rather unusual iced drinks and stirred into fruit salads. Palm fruit seeds have a slightly chewy, jelly-like texture which is most enjoyable when added to ice cream. In the West, they are most commonly available sold in cans or jars steeped in palm sugar syrup. This same palm sugar syrup is used to make jaggery or palm sugar, that is used in all Asian cooking.

recipe using palm fruit seeds, 300 page 177

Carica papaya
Papaya

The papaya or paw-paw, as it is also known, is a wonderful fruit but often people either love it or hate it. It is an acquired taste, very sweet and almost soap-like in its fragrance and very much like a cross between a melon and a peach. Its ripeness is important to enjoy its full potential. Papayas are natives of tropical America and are believed to have reached Europe with the Dutch returning from the East Indies.

These long, oval fruits are generally green and hard when unripe and yellowy-orange, sometimes speckled with green and soft to the touch, when ripe. They have a sweet and aromatic flavour with hot peppery seeds that are scooped out and usually discarded. The skin can vary from yellow or green to red and the fruit is ready to eat when the flesh feels slightly soft when pressed. The skin colour does not always alter as it ripens, so do not rely on this. Cut in half lengthways to reveal the rich yellow, almost coral-coloured flesh with a cluster of small black seeds in the centre, which are believed by the Africans to control fertility. The flesh of the papaya also has strong medicinal properties as it contains a natural painkiller, papaverin.

The best way to enjoy a papaya is to scoop out the seeds from the halved fruit, squeeze a little lime juice all over it and spoon out the ripe, sweet flesh. Not good when cooked, the papaya is best sliced into fruit salads spiced with chilli, and goes well with shellfish and chicken. It also makes an excellent partner to Parma ham, instead of figs or melon.

The hard, unripe green papaya is used shredded in Thai, Cambodian and Vietnamese cooking as a salad ingredient. The juice can be used as a marinade and is great for tenderizing meats. The enzyme papain, present in the flesh, tenderizes meat protein and aids digestion. It also prevents gelatine from setting so do not use in jellies or set mousses.

Since papayas bruise easily, choose uniform-coloured fruits. Check the skin around the stem end; it should be yellow or it will not ripen. Leave to ripen at room temperature and turn frequently.

The skin is inedible, but the seeds can be eaten although they have a very hot peppery taste. They are supposed to be a good cure for stomach upsets. In fact, the papaya is supposed to be an excellent digestive and it is also rich in vitamin A and beta carotene and supplies more than twice an adult's daily requirement of vitamin C. These fruits also contain potassium, fibre and some calcium. They are imported all the year round from Brazil, Jamaica and Ghana.

recipes using papayas, see pages: 101; 131; 147; 150

Carica pentagona
Babacos

Babacos come from the same family as the papaya and look rather like an overgrown papaya. Unlike their cousins, however, babacos have no pips and the skin is edible.

They originated in the Ecuador highlands and have been commercially grown in New Zealand and the Channel Islands since the 1970s. They have five sides, a blunt end, a pointed end and cream or orange flesh. The flavour is not as intense as the papaya and is considered, by some, to be quite bland. When they are under-ripe they are green all over, but with time develop yellow or orange patches. When fully ripe, they will be yellow all over and will need to be used immediately.

Buy them while still unripe and leave them to slowly ripen at room temperature, turning occasionally. Once the fruit is ripe, it will keep in the refrigerator for a couple of days. Like the papaya, the babacos contains the enzyme papain, which is highly beneficial to digestion and also has great culinary advantages as a marinade or tenderizer for meat. It is also high in vitamin C.

The soft flesh is good in fruit salads, or can be thickly sliced and added to savoury salads with goats' cheese and avocado. Alternatively, purée and add to fruit cream syllabubs or fools. To make use of its meat-tenderizing qualities, purée into a marinade for lamb, chicken or pork and then barbecue the meat. Or gently cook diced babacos with lime juice and serve the cooked purée with chicken or roast pork, like an apple sauce accompaniment.

recipe using babacos, see page: 150

Citrullus lanatus
Watermelon

The watermelon is a glorious fruit with its green, mottled or striped, thick skin concealing a brilliant red flesh speckled with little tear-drop black seeds. It is believed to originate from India and Africa and has been enjoyed since ancient times by the Egyptians. It reached Europe around the 13th century when it became a symbol of Italian martyrdom, and is celebrated in Florence with a special festival in August. These fruits can reach a dramatic size or can be quite small and sweet. Look out for the variety Sugar Baby, a round, small melon that is beautifully sweet and juicy. There is also a newcomer, the Mickey Lee variety, which has been bred for its seedless flesh. The yellow variety, called the pinemelon, is a small, pineapple-like fruit exported from Israel.

In general, watermelons are usually round and large but can be more oblong in shape and can be bought in wedges or as halves. When ripe they should yield a little to slight pressure at the top end and when tapped should sound taut and muffled – not hollow. The flesh inside should be red and juicy, full of water. The texture is very different to other melons. It isn't smooth, it is crisper and melts in the mouth. If buying slices, avoid those with white seeds and pale flesh – these will not be sweet as the fruit is unripe.

Watermelons are available from July to September and once cut can be kept in the refrigerator for a week, wrapped in clear film. Since the watermelon contains a lot of watery juice it is low in calories and contains some vitamin B and C. They are at their best served chilled and cut into big wedges.

recipe using watermelon, see page: 170

Citrus grandis
Pomelo

This is the largest of the citrus fruits. It has a thick, dimpled green-yellow skin and is shaped like a flat rugby ball. It looks like a giant misshapen grapefruit, to which it is closely related, but is about twice the size. When pulled apart the fruit contains segments of pink or green flesh, like any citrus fruit each one is surrounded by a bitter, thin skin which is stripped away to enjoy the flesh. It is best to savour each segment by gently popping each one in your mouth to release the sweet juice that oozes out.

The segments are large and slightly coarser than a grapefruit and full of juice sacs that easily tear apart into pieces when preparing. The flesh is deliciously juicy and tangy, yet sweet and refreshing. The edible part of the fruit is probably only half the size of the whole fruit because of the thickness of the pith. It is eaten raw as a fruit or cut up and added to fruit salads or savoury salads with Parma ham, olives and prawns. Originating in South-east Asia, it also pairs well with Asian ingredients like chilli, ginger and Thai fish sauce. It is often used in savoury hot prawn salads and is an excellent accompaniment to hot coconut curries.

It is believed that the pomelo made the journey from Polynesia to the West Indies with a sea captain called Shaddock – hence its second name of Shaddock. It is also known as Adam's apple. The pomelo is now commercially grown outside Asia in Israel and California and is exported worldwide. It has symbolic value to the Vietnamese who use it in their New Year celebrations and a pomelo often takes pride of place on the ancestors' altar in Vietnamese homes. The fruits are in season in late winter and are packed with vitamin C.

recipe using pomelos, see page: 109

Citrus hystrix
Kaffir lime

Kaffir limes are native to Thailand, Cambodia and Vietnam and are grown all over South-east Asia. They are large, bright green limes with a characteristic knobbly and warted skin, and a strong aroma, more powerful than other limes. They have a coarser, less refined flavour that matches the other complex flavours used in the cuisines of South-east Asia. All of the plant is used, from the rind and juice of the fruits to the leaves of the tree. Kaffir lime juice and the finely grated rind are used in marinades, rich curries and seafood soups and are added to all manner of dishes from fish cakes to lime-laced coconut desserts. The juice is also used to make a refreshing drink. They have an astringent aromatic quality and, like the kaffir lime leaves, are used for their distinctive flavour. The leaves are torn, shredded or snipped with scissors and stirred into dishes. They are not eaten but used as a flavouring in the same way that Europeans add bay leaves to their cooking.

 Choose limes that are firm and heavy in the hand and free from blemishes. They will keep in a fruit bowl at room temperature for a week or so and, just before using them, it is well worth warming the limes in a microwave for 20–30 seconds. As with all citrus fruits, this makes squeezing easier and a better extraction of juice. In Thailand the aroma of kaffir limes is believed to ward off evil spirits and the juice is used medicinally. Kaffir limes are available all year round from Asian stores and markets and are packed with vitamin C.

recipes using kaffir limes, see pages: 91; 173

Citrus tangelo
Ugli fruit

True to its name, the poor ugli fruit does not enjoy the beauty of the other members of the citrus family, of which it is a member. This fruit is closely related to the grapefruit and has greeny-yellow, pock-marked skin which is somewhat ill fitting, sack-like and loose. This can be off-putting, but beauty is only skin-deep, as the ugli fruit proves.

Very similar to a grapefruit in flavour, it is sweeter but still has that refreshing tartness and a wonderful juiciness. It is absolutely delicious. Remove the peel and pith and enjoy on its own or use it like a grapefruit, as a starter, sprinkled with brown sugar, in salads or fruit salads or with shellfish. The much-maligned peel can also be candied and used in cakes, ice creams and desserts.

The ugli is available from March to October and is grown commercially in Spain, its country of origin. To choose the best-flavoured fruit, always feel the weight of it before buying. When ripe it should feel firm and heavy for its size. It boasts high vitamin C and beta carotene contents and contains bioflavanoids, which may help to protect against certain forms of cancer. It also contains pectin and potassium. The juice is known to help bruises heal if applied externally.

recipe using ugli fruits, see page: 164

Cocos nucifera
Coconut

Coconuts are natives of the tropics, where they grow along shore lines. They have been used for centuries for their edible flesh, juice and outer husk, that is made into copra rope and matting. The coconuts we immediately recognize are the more mature brown fibrous coconuts with their distinctive large tuft at one end. Inside is the white flesh and at the centre is the hollow that contains the coconut water which makes a refreshing drink. This coconut water is not the same thing as coconut milk. Coconut milk is the juice extracted from the hard white flesh.

Coconuts have three eyes at one end and when the coconut is shaken it is possible to hear the coconut water sloshing around inside. The quickest way to get inside a coconut is to take a corkscrew and screw it into each of the eyes in turn. The coconut water can be poured out of the holes and drunk. Then with a hammer tap all the way around the middle of the coconut, repeating and repeating, until eventually the coconut naturally breaks in half along its fault. Failing that, drop it on a clean stone

surface. Prise the coconut flesh from the shell and, using a potato peeler, remove and discard the thick brown skin. The white flesh is now ready to use. Use the potato peeler once again to make large shavings to decorate puddings and cakes or chop or grate the flesh to use in recipes.

The green coconut, or jelly coconut, is a young coconut that has not yet developed the thick white flesh. If a green coconut is opened, it has a thin covering of opaque, jelly-like flesh and plenty of coconut water. These coconuts are harvested for drinking. The liquid is very refreshing and no matter where you are coconut water can be drunk without any risk of water-borne diseases.

A good test when buying a coconut is to shake it. They dry out as they get older, so the less water the drier the flesh will be. To make coconut milk, grate the flesh, cover with boiling water and leave to stand until cold. Mash with the hands to dissolve as much of the oil and juices into the water as possible and then pass through a cloth or muslin, squeezing out as much juice as you can. This is now ready to use in coconut desserts, curries and soups. Coconuts are rich in oil and vitamins A and D.

recipes using coconuts, see pages: 116; 129; 157

Cucumis metuliferus
Kiwiano

The kiwiano is a bizarre fruit to look at – almost prehistoric. On first acquaintance, it is not obvious whether it is a fruit or a vegetable, let alone what is inside. It has a thick, bright orange skin covered in spiky, short horns and, like a passion fruit, it is packed with transparent melon-like seeds that are a translucent green colour. It is also known as the jelly melon, African horned melon, or the horned cucumber for its faint cucumber flavour.

The kiwiano is part of the cucumber family and originates in Africa but is now grown commercially in Portugal, the USA and New Zealand, from where its name was developed, to cash in on the country's association with the kiwi fruit and, of course, to raise its profile. It has no relationship or similarity with the kiwi fruit except that both fruits are green on the inside.

When cut in half, the inedible skin reveals hundreds of seeds like a melon, each one covered in a jelly-like pulp, which has a range of complex flavours including melon, cucumber, banana and lime. Eat the seeds and pulp spooned over ice cream and desserts or add to salads with cucumber or tomato and salty cheese such as feta. Alternatively, make into a refreshing drink blended with sugar syrup or with yogurt and honey. These fruits are rich in vitamin C and are available from October to March.

recipe using kiwiano, see page: 104

Cydonia oblonga
Quince

Quince are natives of western Asia and grow on a small tree with low twisted branches and large aromatic white flowers. These ancient fruit, greatly appreciated by the Greeks and Romans, arrived in Europe from the east around the 10th century. They are beautiful lobe-shaped fruits with a golden yellow skin and a dry, almost pear-like flesh. Highly aromatic, even though they are not a juicy fruit, they are rarely eaten uncooked and are usually made into a purée and served with game or pork or cooked into a preserve as a jam or jelly and served with strong meats like wild boar and venison. They are also cooked in desserts, particularly with apples, with which they have a strong affinity. A few slices of quince added to an apple pie will lift the flavour with their heady aroma. As the flesh cooks it takes on a pink tinge.

The quince is one of the earliest fruits known to man and has been linked with love and fertility, myth has it that Aphrodite, the goddess of love, accepted a quince from her lover Paris. The humble quince symbolizes the fruits of love and marriage and is often served at weddings in Greece and other Latin countries. They are rarely seen in shops and are mostly available through the autumn months and, if stored correctly, well into winter. The flesh can be cooked with sugar to a pulp to create a quince cheese, an old English recipe that is also known in Spain, where it is called *membrillo*. Left to cool and set, it is served thickly sliced, in particular with the Spanish sheep's cheese, *Manchego*.

To prepare, wash off the grey down that covers the outside. Cut the quince in half, peel and core and drop the flesh into a bowl of water with half a lemon squeezed into it. This prevents the quince from browning. The flesh oxidizes on contact with air and turns brown quickly.

Cyphomandra betacea
Tamarillo

The tamarillo is a strange looking fruit indeed, a fruit that makes one wonder who first discovered that it was edible? Originally from South America and now grown throughout the tropics and many sub-tropical countries, the fruit is like a tomato in appearance, taste and use. It is about 8 cm (3 inches) long and oval in shape. The tamarillo is also known as the java plum or the tree tomato, since it grows on bushes and looks very like an elongated plum tomato. The thin, inedible skin is smooth but tough and orangey-red, a bit like a painted egg. If ripe, the fruit should give a little when gently pressed. Peel the skin off, or cut in half and scoop out the glorious-coloured flesh, which closely resembles a cross between a plum and a tomato. Eaten raw, however, the tamarillo is extremely acidic, so bitter it puts a film on your teeth even when fully ripe. The best way to enjoy them is to bake them or poach them in a sweet syrup, then peel away the skin. Serve chilled or warm with a creamy sauce. They can also be spiced and baked or grilled and served as a vegetable with fish or poultry, or made into pickles and jams.

recipe using tamarillos, see page: 162

Diospyros kaki
Persimmon

The persimmon, or Sharon fruit, looks like a great orange tomato but with a wide brown calyx. The commercially available variety of persimmon was specially bred by the Israelis and derives from the Sharon Valley, where it is still grown, hence the name. Also known as the date plum, the original persimmons were natives of Japan and China and their Japanese name means 'food of the gods'. In ancient China the persimmon was eaten to relieve hangovers and was also enjoyed dried as a candied sweet.

The Sharon fruit variety is much sweeter than its parent persimmon and tastes a little like a combination of melon and peach. Although the smooth orange skin is edible, it is best peeled off to fully enjoy the dense, sweet and luscious flesh that is a glistening orange colour with flavour tones of pumpkin, plum and a hint of vanilla.

Slice horizontally to reveal the highly decorative star-shaped seeded centre and use in fruit salads, cheesecakes and flans or in a pavlova. Sharon fruits benefit from a squeeze of lime juice. They are also good in savoury salads, in particular with avocado. Keep for a few days until the fruit ripens fully and becomes deliciously soft, then try chilling it in the refrigerator for a while, slice off the top and scoop out the juicy flesh with a spoon. They should be plump and heavy in the hand with perfect unblemished skins since they can bruise easily. To ripen quickly, put in a paper bag with a banana and give it a warm afternoon or a day to mature. Sharon fruit provides half the recommended daily intake of vitamin A, plus potassium, calcium, iron and some vitamin C. They are available between November and April.

recipe using persimmons, see page: 161

Durio zibethinus
Durian

The durian is a great delicacy and one of the most intriguing exotic fruits. It originated in Malaysia and spread across South-east Asia during prehistoric times and is now also grown in East Africa. The durian is legendary for its creamy pulp, but its pungent aroma is an acquired taste. The durian is the one fruit that is not allowed on aeroplanes and is strapped to the tops of vehicles since its smell is so obnoxious, redolent of drains and rotting matter. There is a curious obsession with this fruit, which may have more to do with the belief that it is an aphrodisiac. It is said that elephants and tigers are rather partial to it, too. It grows on a tree and forms a thick wood-like skin covered with an armour-plating of stubby sharp spikes. Underneath this yellow, green or brown skin are three to five large segments of creamy white pulp, the texture of custard. The intense flavour is sweet and reminiscent of a curious mixture of many tropical fruits. Each segment contains several large shiny, black seeds.

The durian is best eaten raw and straight from the market stall. It is essential to eat durians very fresh and it is advisable not to keep them, although the pulp can be frozen and is then virtually odourless. A yellowing of the skin indicates ripeness. If the skin is damaged, don't buy it. Cut through the tough skin at the segment joints, press out the segments and scoop out the lobe-like flesh and seed. The rich custardy flesh is eaten as it is or added to ice cream. The seeds can be roasted and are also eaten in curries or chutneys. The durian is a starchy fruit which provides a good source of vitamin C and potassium. The pungent aroma can be quite off-putting but it is well worth trying – outdoors.

Euphorbia longana
Longan

Longans look very similar to lychees and grow in profusion from the overladen branches of the longan tree. The skin of the longan is smoother than that of the lychee and not warty or scaly like its cousin. Longans, or dragons' eyes as they are also called, are slightly larger than lychees and are round with a pale brown outer casing. They have a brittle skin that is peeled away, under which the jewel-like fleshy fruit awaits. Like the lychee, the translucent perfumed flesh is held around a central inedible stone. They taste very similar to lychees, with a sweet, aromatic juicy flavour, but with an added peppery tang. The longan tree is native to China and grows throughout South-east Asia and China. The fruit can be eaten raw or added to sweet and sour dishes. When first picked, the skin is a delicate shade of orange and slightly furry but within a day or so this colour disappears and the skin turns brown.

Choose fruits that are unblemished and heavy for their size. This will mean that they have plenty of juice. They will keep in the bottom of the refrigerator for a week or so and can be eaten as a fresh fruit or added to fruit salads. They can also be served with Parma ham and smoked meats or alongside Chinese dishes. They are packed with vitamin C and are in season in late summer.

recipe using longans, see page: 106

Feijoas

Feijoas are native to South America and are named after the Portuguese botanist Dom da Silva Feijoa who discovered them in Brazil and brought them to the attention of Europe. The feijoa is now commercially grown in New Zealand, Israel and South and North America. It is also known as pineapple guava or guavasteen.

It tastes like an aromatic strawberry and is a distant member of the guava family. Feijoas have a rich scent and a crisp, sharp-tasting flesh. When unripe, the skin is green and the fruit tastes like a banana but as it ripens the skin turns a mottled red-green or yellow colour and the flesh becomes more aromatic. The creamy-white flesh is slightly jelly-like and the fruit contains many hard seeds at its centre. The seeds are inedible and should be scooped out and discarded.

Feijoas are best eaten raw, by cutting in half and simply eating the sweet flesh with a spoon and a squeeze of lime juice. Alternatively, slice the juicy flesh and use to top fresh fruit tarts or add to a simple melon and grapefruit salad. In South America, the flesh is also made into a preserve. Feijoas are packed with vitamin C and are also rich in iodine.

Ficus carica
Fig

The dusky fig is synonymous with the Mediterranean where it grows through the long warm days to a succulent ripeness. These fruits are, however, native to Syria. They are principally grown in Brazil, Turkey, Greece and the Middle East and are sold virtually all year round. However, they are primarily in season in the summer and autumn and are otherwise available dried. They are luscious fruits that are entirely edible – the skin, flesh and seeds. There are several varieties which vary in colour from grape-black through to green and yellow and even white. The best known are the black mission fig from Mexico and California, the kadota, a green fig from Greece and Italy, and the sari lob from Cyprus and Israel. There is also a reddish-brown variety called Brown Turkey that grows easily in Britain and fruits well.

Choose firm yet slightly soft figs and cut open just before eating to reveal the succulent red or purple centre full of sweet seeds. These succulent fruits are ideal with both savoury and sweet dishes. They are added to Mediterranean salads with feta cheese, olives, Parma ham, smoked meats and rocket or can be sliced and added to fruit salads and open tarts, or open sandwiches with soft cheese. They are delicious slowly poached in wine in the oven and served with almond biscuits. They are also used to make preserves. Figs contain vitamin B and are full of fibre.

recipe using figs, see page: 154

Fortunella japonica
Kumquat

Kumquats are synonymous with China, and during the Chinese New Year these little orange fruits, no bigger than an olive, symbolize good fortune. During this festival, to improve their lot, the Chinese decorate their houses with kumquat and orange trees in full fruit.

Their skin resembles that of an orange, only it is much thinner. The skin is edible and tastes and smells distinctly orangey. You can usually find kumquats in the shops from January onwards, but despite their more frequent appearance these days, people are still wary of what to do with them. You can eat the whole thing, skin, pith and all, although they can be quite tart and full of seeds that need spitting out. A more popular way of eating them is to cook them with game, poultry or fish to enhance the flavour of the meats. The fruits then become soft, pulpy and more palatable. If you do eat them raw they have a glorious fragrance of oranges and orange blossom, which seems to permeate the mouth with a refreshing zingy energy. Like most citrus fruits, they are rich in vitamin C and are equally good in sweet and savoury dishes.

recipe using kumquats, see page: 144

Garcinia mangostana
Mangosteen

The mangosteen is not related in any way to the mango, despite its name. This is clear from its appearance, which is as different from the smooth plump mango as you can get. These highly exotic fruits are natives of South-east Asia and grow on trees that take fifteen years to reach fruiting stage – but the wait is worth it.

A mangosteen is the size of a large plum or small apple; it has a hard crinkled, almost leathery brown skin with a purplish hue. This skin is totally inedible and full of bright staining pink juice that oozes out and colours hands and clothes alike. The thick central stalk has curled leaves. Inside this protective encasement is a real treasure. Peel away the thick skin and pith with care to reveal the beautiful pearl-like segments of the fruit itself. The flavour is a rare and exotic treat, sweet and luscious with a slight acidity and a heady scent. To eat, simply cut round the top with a sharp knife, as the skin is quite thick for the size of the fruit, and scoop out the flesh from the segments with a teaspoon, discarding the inedible stones. This fruit needs nothing else to enhance it and, to be fully enjoyed, it should be eaten on its own. It is still a relatively rare fruit, but it can be found in some specialist and Asian shops and is worth seeking out.

Hylocereus undatus & Hylocereus polyhizus
Dragon fruit & Pithaya

These rather prehistoric-looking fruits are natives of Mexico and are also grown in Vietnam and Israel. They are available from March to December and are either bright fuchsia-pink in colour or yellow, when they are better known as pithaya.

The name dragon fruit originates from the series of small leaf scars on both the pink and yellow fruits which are thought to resemble dragon scales.

When cut in half the dragon fruit reveals a juicy white flesh and thousands of tiny edible black seeds, the size of small sesame seeds. These succulent cactus fruits have a mild-flavoured, watery flesh that is lightly perfumed and not unlike an unsweet melon. The flesh is crisp and juicy like a kiwi. Choose fruits that are slightly soft when gently squeezed and, once they have reached this stage, they can be kept in the refrigerator for a couple of days.

These exotic fruits look and taste rather unusual and are probably best appreciated when eaten as a fresh fruit, served with a lemon sorbet or added to an exotic fruit salad with melon. Lime and lemon juice are often squeezed on to the flesh just before serving to enhance the flavour. Dragon fruits and pithaya are best served chilled. They are rich in vitamin C and fibre.

Litchi chinensis
Lychees

Lychees are beautiful little oriental fruits with a pinkish-brown, rough, scaly, hard skin that splits and peels away easily. Underneath is a pearl – a juicy white and highly aromatic fruit, delicately perfumed, around an inedible seed. The flesh is soft and crisp and oozes a delicious sweet juice. Lychees have been cultivated in China for centuries and are a Chinese symbol of romance. Old Chinese stories tell of one of the Emperor's concubines insisting on the fruit being brought hundreds of miles for her personal consumption.

Their aromatic flavour, a little like a muscat grape, is feverishly popular in China, where barrows of the fruits are consumed during their long season. They are available most of the year, except in March and April, and are now grown commercially for the worldwide market in Africa, New Zealand, the Far East and South America. It is worth checking lychees before buying, since they do dry out quickly. To choose the sweetest fruits, look for the pinkest skin. The brittle skins should be unblemished, a pink or brown colour, and feel quite heavy for their size. This will mean they are packed with juice. If they are very brown, this tends to mean they are past their best. They will keep at room temperature for a few days and in the refrigerator for up to a week.

Lychees are traditionally served at the end of a Chinese meal, particularly in restaurants, and are ideal eaten on their own or added to fruit salads, ice creams or stuffed with cream cheese and nuts. They also team well with pork and duck and can be poached in a lime or orange syrup and served with little almond or saffron biscuits. They are rich in vitamin C.

recipes using lychees, see pages: 137; 146; 153

Mangifera indica
Mango

You can find mangoes of almost every shape, size and colour from the tiniest, heart-shaped yellow mango to the largest, oval mango with its red-flushed skin. They originated in the Far East, India and South-east Asia. The Portuguese introduced them to Brazil from where they spread into the rest of tropical South America and Central America, the Caribbean and Florida. They are also commercially grown in East and West Africa.

The mango is a fragrant and juicy fruit with about 2500 varieties ranging from large, ball-shaped fruits to those the size of a lemon, which are often green and used in India for making chutney. Although they are relative newcomers to the West, they are readily available and can be bought almost all year round.

Mangoes are succulent and have a flavour that is a cross between a peach and a melon, with a hint of pineapple – very tropical and a highly exotic mix. Choose mangoes that are heavy in the hand, firm yet soft and that do not have any dark patches. A ripe fruit should yield to slight pressure and the orange-yellow flesh should be sweet and smooth and oozing with juice. Don't be deceived by the colour of the skin. Some mangoes are ripe when the skin is still green, others have a rich red flush, others are pale yellow. Eating a mango is a messy but extremely pleasurable business. A good mango should not be too fibrous, but some varieties are more so than others. To serve, cut a vertical slice either side of the stone and score the flesh in each half into cubes. Bend the skin back to separate the cubes, then

spoon or slice the flesh into a bowl. The mango is rich in vitamin C, beta carotene (which the body converts into vitamin A) and antioxidants. One medium mango provides more than the recommended daily intake of vitamin C. It is also high in sugar.

The mango is a delicious fruit served on its own or freshly chopped and mixed with red onion as a salsa with meat. It can also be puréed and mixed into cream as a fool or added to ice cream and sorbets. It is also good in salads.

recipes using mangoes, see pages: 138; 152; 161; 168

Manilkara
achras sapota
Sapodilla

The sapodilla is an unassuming fruit that is a native of Central America but now grows all over South-east Asia. The oval fruits with their buff, slightly rough skin look very like potatoes and grow on a huge tree that is overladen with fruit. This same tree also yields chicle, a latex sap that is tapped from the bark in much the same way as rubber is in rubber plantations. The chicle sap is then processed and becomes, of all things, chewing gum.

The sapodilla fruit or chico, as it is known in India, is far removed from chewing gum in flavour. The skin of a ripe sapodilla should be slightly wrinkled and give a little when pressed. If unripe, the fruits are green and hard with a strange grainy texture and an unpleasant mouth-puckering flavour. As they reach ripeness the skin turns a lovely yellow-orange colour. The flesh is a golden honey-orange, similar to a guava, with an aromatic flavour of vanilla and bananas. It has shiny black seeds at the centre which should be scooped out and discarded.

The sapodilla should be enjoyed, quite simply, as it is. Scoop the flesh out of the inedible skin with a spoon and add a squeeze of lime to enhance the flavour. In India, the vanilla and banana flavour is used to great advantage by whizzing the flesh into milkshakes with cumin or cardamom seeds.

Sapodillas are full of vitamins C and A and also contain fibre. Ripe fruits will keep in the refrigerator for a week or two while unripe fruits can be left to ripen at room temperature. They are available most of the year.

recipe using sapodillas, see page: 172 **37**

Musa sapientium
Apple banana

This dwarf finger banana is the smallest of the banana family and has a very thin skin and buttery yellow flesh when ripe. As its name suggests, it has a subtle apple flavour, which is faintly flowery, and a firm fibrous texture. It is sweeter than conventional bananas and is a perfect size for a quick snack and for children to eat. In general, bananas are one of the most everyday tropical fruits available and are perfect for their slow-release energy and high quantities of potassium. They also contain B vitamins and plenty of fibre – which makes them the perfect convenience food.

Bananas have grown in South-east Asia since ancient times. On the island of Sumatra in Indonesia, the everyday street food *Pisang goreng* is made with local bananas that contain small dark stones at the tip. These are the banana seeds that have been bred out of commercial bananas.

Buy apple bananas while still slightly green and allow to ripen at room temperature. Like any bananas, do not buy if they are slightly brown as this shows they are ripe, if not over-ripe. Look for those with slightly green tips. If the skin is speckled and mottled with brown patches, the banana will be ripe and soft and best for mashing with cream or yogurt or making into banana smoothies. When keeping bananas it is well worth remembering two things: bananas in a fruit bowl will ripen all the other fruit – so beware. And never store them in the refrigerator – this makes the skin blacken.

Eat them as they come or add them sliced to sponge puddings and cakes. If you have plenty of bananas that are all ripening at the same stage, peel, slice and freeze them. Use them later for smoothies, when the frozen chunks can be added to the blender with yogurt. You won't need ice.

recipes using apple bananas, see pages: 165; 169

Nephelium lappaceum
Rambutan

This very strange, hairy little fruit is a relative of the lychee, although you wouldn't think so from its outside appearance. It is larger than a lychee, about the size of a plum, and is covered in a mass of curved, quite fearsome-looking, but soft, ruby-red spines. The rambutan, or hairy lychee as it is also known, originated in Malaysia and is now grown in Central and North America and South-east Asia. These juicy little fruits are great favourites in South-east Asia and are eaten by the bagload when they are in full season. In Thailand there is even a rambutan festival and a rambutan queen crowned in honour of this curious-looking fruit.

Break open the brittle, spiny skin and the translucent, succulent white flesh reveals its link with the lychee. In taste and texture it closely resembles the lychee – sweet, juicy and fragrant, but with a slightly sharper tone. Like the lychee, it also has a central, inedible, shiny black stone. A decorative way to present this fruit is to cut around the middle of the hairy coat with a sharp knife and then pull off the top section of skin to leave the white flesh nestled in its cup of hairy spines. These fruits look inviting for breakfast but are also delicious served with Parma ham or smoked meats for a light lunch. Generally rambutans are eaten in the same way as lychees, by removing the flesh from the stone and eating it raw, straight from the skin. It can also be served in a delicate syrup on its own or with other exotic fruits or in ice cream or fools. Like the lychee, the rambutan is rich in vitamin C. It is imported from Thailand and Indonesia from March to October.

recipes using rambutans, see pages: 105; 153

Opuntia ficus-indica

Prickly pear

This cactus fruit is native to Mexico and South America and grows prolifically in hot, arid locations. The prickly pear or cactus pear is a cactus fruit and is covered in many tiny needle-like hairs. These are the classic South American fruits but are also grown in North and South Africa, Colombia, Israel, Italy and Spain.

The prickly pear is also known as the Indian or Barbary fig and is generally oval in shape and about 10 cm (4 inches) long, with a greenish-orange skin when ripe. Choose firm fruits and allow them to ripen slowly at room temperature. Once ripe the skin should give a little when pressed but beware of the prickles. Many stores have these prickles removed prior to selling but it is still advisable to wear plastic gloves when preparing the fruit.

Inside, the fruit is sweet and succulent with small chewy edible seeds and the flesh can be either red, pink or yellow. When the fruit is ripe the skin turns an orange-red colour and yields slightly when pressed. At this stage, either cut in half and scoop out the sweet and aromatic flesh, or cut the top off, cut down one side and ease the whole fruit out and then cut it in half, slice or dice it. To further enjoy the sweet, dense flavour, a squeeze of lime juice enhances its characteristic tones.

Prickly pears are available all year round and contrast well with other fruits. They are good in fruit salads, in particular with oranges, and make a rich conserve. They are also good added to savoury salads and eaten with salty cheese like feta or haloumi.

recipe using prickly pears, see page: 110

Passiflora edulis
Passion fruit

The passion fruit is a delectable little fruit, no larger than a plum and of the same shape, with a purple-black skin that becomes more wrinkled as it ripens. Cut the fruit in half and inside the pith-lined shell is the deeply fragrant pulp. Lots of little black seeds, which are crunchy to the bite, are covered in the sweet, juicy yellowy-orange flesh. The best way to enjoy the passion fruit is simply to spoon out the pulp and eat it just as it is. It is no good when cooked as all the flavour and fragrance is lost, but in sorbets, mousses, soufflés or in fruit salads the sweet, perfumed taste of the passion fruit is incomparable. You can also strain the juice through a sieve to extract the seeds and use the juice in cocktails and other drinks and jellies.

Native to South America, the passion fruit is now grown commercially in Australia, Africa and some south-eastern states of America and these days can be found in most shops and food markets. It is a healthy source of vitamin C, vitamins B2 and B5 and is an ideal way to start the day. Serve the passion fruit in an egg cup with the top sliced off and spoon out the delicious pulp. Some sugar might be required.

recipes using passion fruits, see pages: 158; 170

Passiflora ligularis
Grenadilla

The grenadilla is a native of South America and is a close relative of the passion fruit. It is the largest of the passion fruit family and is less fragrant than a standard passion fruit, with a sweet yet tart flavour. It looks highly elegant with its perfectly round shape and long, thin stalk that stands straight upwards from the orange mottled skin.

A grenadilla is light when held in the hand and has a skin that feels like an eggshell. When choosing a grenadilla, remember that the fruit is ripe when the skin changes colour from orange to yellow. They will keep at room temperature for a day or so, or can be chilled in the refrigerator for up to a week. Beneath the thin, brittle shell there is a thick spongy white membrane, and then the numerous edible seeds and pulp at its centre. To serve, cut off the stalk end like the top of a boiled egg and scoop out the seeds and flesh with a teaspoon or simply eat from the shell. Eat as it is, for breakfast or a snack, or serve with yogurt or crème fraîche. Mix into a fool or a light custard to make an exotic trifle. When cut, the inedible, brittle skin cracks easily so if the shell is to be used for presentation use the point of a sharp knife and carefully cut round the fruit.

Grenadillas are full of vitamin C and are available all year round imported from Colombia.

Passiflora mollissima
Curuba

Known as the banana passion fruit because of its shape, this is one of those strange-looking exotic fruits. It is elongated, rather like a chubby finger, with a thin central stalk. The skin is yellow with a hint of green. When cut in half, the curuba has a similar collection of seeds and pulp as a regular passion fruit. The seeds have a sharp, sweet flavour and the pulp is orange and very tart, similar to the passion fruit but with a more powerful flavour. It can be difficult to find but is very popular in its native Colombia. Serve with a little sugar to overcome the tartness. It is very good in fruit salads and sorbets and can be used in much the same way as a passion fruit in desserts and drinks.

Date Phoenix dactylifera

Dates are the fruits of the Old World – Israel, Turkey and the Middle East. These pods of super-sweet pulp are great favourites through the winter months and are frequently used in baking and Middle Eastern cooking. Records show that they have been cultivated for at least 5000 years. The ancient Greeks and Romans ate them in abundance and added them to their dishes.

Dates grow on the tall, slender date palm (tree of life) on lots of small branches that hang from the central core of the palm. They generally grow in sub-tropical and desert areas of North Africa, Arabia, California and Australasia.

There are many varieties of date and countries of origin. Those with the strongest flavour are the Egyptian medjool dates which are sticky, plump, moist and very sweet. The deglet nour from North Africa have a superior flavour that is almost chocolaty, while the halawi dates from Israel are often coated in a glucose syrup and are quite dry by comparison. Israeli hayani dates are plump, fresh tasting and very moist but are not as flavoursome as some. Many of the hayani dates will have been frozen which means that the flavour is not as concentrated.

Dates contain an oval stone at their centre, which needs to be removed before the flesh is used in recipes. Dried dates are used in a variety of sweet and savoury dishes from fruit cakes and steamed sponges to Moroccan tagines and pastries. They are excellent dried fruits for compôtes and for adding to cheese boards or fruit bowls. They are packed with sugar and fibre and are also a good supply of potassium and trace minerals.

recipe using dates, see page: 149

Physalis peruviana
Physalis

Physalis, also known as the Peruvian cherry, is a tiny little orange-coloured fruit about the size and shape of a gooseberry, but with a little lantern-shaped papery husk, inspiring its name of Chinese lantern. Native to South America, these fruits were also eaten by the Greeks back in the 3rd century. They came to England in the 18th century but took time to become popular. They were taken with the early settlers to South Africa, here they were cultivated in the Cape of Good Hope, hence their other name of Cape gooseberry.

Inside the smooth skin are hundreds of little seeds. To eat them, you simply peel back the inedible papery husk and bite into the fruit. They have a very strange, mildly scented, sweet and sour flavour. Although they can be eaten raw, they are best turned into jams, compôtes and sauces. Slightly tart, they are also delicious dipped in sugar before popping in the mouth, or dipped into a fondant icing flavoured with a liqueur. Because it is such a pretty fruit to look at, it can be used as a wonderful garnish or served with petits fours at the end of a meal. Available during February and March.

recipes using physalis, see pages: 161; 166

Psidium guajava
Guava

A soft-skinned, pale yellow, pear-shaped fruit, usually the size of an apple, the guava is a magical fruit with the most exquisite juice. Coming from Central and South America, the Caribbean and Thailand, these fruits are not widely used, perhaps because of their unusual, somewhat musky fragrance similar to that of a quince. Because of this fragrance, it is best to store guavas away from other foods.

The flesh is either white or pink, soft and grainy, with a highly aromatic flavour, sweet yet quite tart, and contains numerous flat crunchy seeds. The smaller and pinker the fruits are, the better and more highly flavoured, although these days those available in the shops are usually green and quite large, so they need to be ripened before eating. They are fragile and should be handled with care to prevent bruising.

To eat, cut in half, sprinkle with lime or lemon juice and eat with a spoon, discarding the skin. Ice creams, sorbets, jams and jellies can be made with guava, and it also combines well with apples in sauces for meat, game and poultry. Or gently poach in a light syrup and serve with crème fraîche. The juice is wonderful, creamy and green and can be used in cocktails. It is rich in beta carotene, vitamins B3 and C, calcium and potassium. These fruits are grown commercially in Brazil and Egypt and are available through the autumn and winter months.

recipe using guavas, see page: 169

Punica granatum
Pomegranate

Pomegranates originated in Persia and have been popular in the Middle East for centuries. They are highly regarded as a symbol of fertility since Venus, the goddess of love, was said to have much prized the fruit as presents for her loved ones. They are used in cooking throughout the Middle East and are now cultivated in France, the Mediterranean, Israel, the USA and all over Asia. As they arrive in the West in September, they herald the start of the festive season and stay the course through the winter and into early summer the next year. They have autumnal colours too, a thick burnished gold leathery skin with tinges of crimson, yellows and brown. They are prone to scarring and occasional brown patches, but this does not affect the flesh or flavour.

Inside, the gem-like seeds with their juicy red or crimson flesh are packed in tightly in small groups, separated by a thin, bitter membrane. Children enjoy picking the seeds out one-by-one, but if you don't have that child-like time and patience, cut the skin into segments, then peel back the skin and ease out the seeds into a bowl, being careful not to include any of the pith. Another way is to hold the cut half of the pomegranate firmly over a bowl and smack the outside with a wooden spoon until the seeds tumble out. If the juice is required, roll the fruit in the hand for a couple of minutes, squeezing and pummelling it gently. Then when the skin is carefully pierced, the juice should flow freely. The seeds themselves can be used for decorating bruschetta, salads, curries, tagines and desserts and are included in many Middle Eastern recipes. The juice is superb, too, and can be used in marinades or for flavouring drinks, ices and syrups. They are rich in vitamin C.

recipe using pomegranates, see page: 148   **47**

Pyrus pyrifolia
Nashi pear

The nashi pear, or Japanese pear, is a firm, white-fleshed, very aromatic and juicy fruit. It is indigenous to China and Japan and looks rather lovely with perfect yellow to rosy pink hues and a shape like a large round pear, a little bit like a quince. During his travels through China, Marco Polo was one of the first Europeans to taste a nashi pear and remarked on its succulence and distinctive flavour.

Also known as the snow pear, it has a somewhat delicate appearance, looking more like an apple than a pear. Its texture is crisp and watery, but not highly juicy, with an aromatic semi-sweet flavour. Its texture is more akin to an apple than a pear with none of the grainy European pear texture.

Choose nashi pears that are firm, have a delicate fragrant aroma and are unblemished. Eat the whole fruit raw like one would a pear, or slice and add to savoury or sweet salads or add to grated salads with daikon radish and small sweet carrots. Gently poach or simmer thick slices of nashi and make into a sauce for duck, pork or chicken, or cook whole around or stuffed inside a goose or duck like quince or apples. In China they often eat the sliced flesh with salt. They are available during the winter months and are rich in vitamin A and fibre.

recipe using nashi pears, see page: 98

Solanum muricatum
Pepino

The pepino, also known as the tree melon, is a native of Peru and has a smooth golden skin streaked with purple-red markings. These fruits look like small oval melons and grow on a herbaceous bush. They are members of the Solanaceae family, like the tomato, potato and aubergine.

The flesh is pale yellow with a tart, lemony flavour with hints of melon and pineapple. The seeds are also edible and are sweetly flavoured. To enjoy this fruit, simply cut in half, peel away the skin, remove the seeds and eat raw. They are rich in vitamin C and contain some vitamin A. Pepinos are also good poached in a light sugar syrup and served with ice cream, other fruits and sorbets or just sliced and eaten in savoury salads with avocado and smoked hams.

Agaricus bisporus
Oriental mushrooms

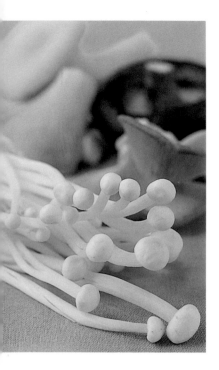

China has been using mushrooms for approximately 2000 years and 858 species grow within its vast territory. Oriental mushrooms include enoki, shiitake and oyster, all of which are becoming more and more popular for both their health-giving and edible qualities. If mushrooms are bought fresh and kept cool, they will last for 4–5 days. Keep them wrapped in paper in the bottom of the refrigerator, but with time they will oxidize and turn dark. Never wash a mushroom, just wipe with a barely damp cloth or piece of kitchen paper. Generally mushrooms contain 80 per cent water, some carbohydrate, protein, B vitamins, iron and minerals.

Shiitake mushrooms (*Lentinus edodes*) originated in Japan and are closely related to the Chinese black mushroom. They are the most commonly used oriental mushrooms and the second most cultivated in the world. They have large, brown to black, umbrella-shaped caps and are available fresh or dried. If dried, soak for 30 minutes in hot water before using. They are grown in both China and Japan on dead shii trees, from which they take their name. They can also grow on oak and are then known as oak mushrooms. These are fragrant mushrooms with a distinctive meaty and smoky oak flavour. They provide an excellent source of protein and are used in Japan as a meat substitute. Their impressive medical qualities help to reduce cholesterol and blood pressure and also produce Interfern, an antiviral agent. Interestingly, in the battle against cancer and Aids, the Japanese have created an approved drug, Lentinan, which improves the rate of survival and is made using compounds from the shiitake mushroom. Nutritionally it contains all the amino acids and a blend of vitamins A, B, C, D and niacin and has a fat-absorbing compound.

Oyster mushrooms (*Pleurotus ostreatus*) are silky grey, oyster-brown, yellow or pink and have a delicate flavour and texture. They are highly desired in all oriental cooking. They grow on decaying stumps in beautiful fans of irregular oval lobes. They were first recorded in Europe in the 17th century in Austria and Hungary and now are cultivated in Europe, northern China and Japan. They have a delicate seafood flavour and contain vitamins B1 and B6, potassium, folic acid and sulphur.

Enoki (*Flammulina velutipes*) are creamy-white mushrooms, with long slender stems topped with pin-like caps. They grow in bunches on the stumps of the enoki (Chinese hackberry) tree and require trimming to separate them. They have a mild flavour, crisp texture and are slightly sweet to taste. They can be eaten fresh or cooked and are available all year round. They contain sodium, vitamin C and iron.

Cloud ear fungus (*Auricularia polytricha*) have been used in Chinese cooking since the 6th century and are highly regarded for their cleansing and blood-purifying properties. They have a delicate flavour and crunchy bite and are sold dried. On soaking, they expand to five times their dried size and do not require much cooking – use in soups, stir-fries and braised dishes.

recipe using oriental mushrooms, see page: 88

Algae
sp. laminaria digitata
Sea vegetables

Seaweed is the prize vegetable of the sea and is harvested off the coasts of Asia from unpolluted waters. It is mostly eaten in Japan where kombu and nori seaweeds are best known as additions to miso soups and sushi. They are extremely nutritious and high in iron, calcium, magnesium and vitamin D. It is suggested that seaweed should be included in everyone's diet for its nutritional qualities. When cooking dried beans or grains, add kombu or wakame to the water to improve the balance of iodine, iron, copper, zinc and selenium trace nutrients. Kombu can be made into tea and drunk three times a week, while nori sheets are an ideal snack instead of crisps, and should be eaten a few times a week.

Hijiki (*Cystphyllum fusiforme*) are thin strands of black seaweed that look like loose tea. It grows in Japanese waters and is sold dried. When soaked, it expands to three times its original size. It has a nutty taste and is used in stir-fries and soups.

Kombu (*Laminaria japonica*) is a giant sea kelp used in dashi, the basic miso soup base. It is primarily gathered off the island of Hokkaido in Japan. It is deep olive green in colour and full of the flavour of the sea. It is sold in its dry form and develops a salty white mould on storage that requires wiping off with a damp cloth. Soak in warm water until soft, score the surface and simmer for 30 minutes to make a stock base.

Nori (*Pophyra tenera*) is a type of marine algae harvested from Japan's surface waters. It is used to make agar-agar, the vegetarian setting agent. Dried and pressed into paper-thin sheets, it varies from black to bright green and is used as a wrapper for sushi. It is also available shredded and mixed with seeds and is used as a condiment on rice, fish and chicken. Nori sheets are sometimes sold pre-toasted or can be toasted until crisp over a flame.

Wakame (*Undavia pinnatifida*) is deep green to brown and belongs to the brown algae family. It looks very similar to wood ear fungus and is used chopped into fine pieces in many Japanese dishes. The green varieties are used in Chinese and Korean cooking in soups and salads while the brown types, known as arame, are less delicate in flavour and texture.

recipes using sea vegetables, see pages: 86; 88

Allium ampeloprasum
Elephant garlic

Elephant garlic is one of the newest and largest garlics available commercially and is mainly exported from Oregon in the north-west of the USA. Originally garlic was grown in Central Asia but is now grown throughout the world, in particular in Asia, the USA and the Mediterranean. An ancient plant, it was used for its culinary and healing properties as far back as the early days of the Egyptians, Greeks and Romans. Even Aristotle believed it to be a cure for rabies. It is a perennial bulb, part of the onion family, but these particular heads of elephant garlic have dimensions closer to a large white onion. If you hold a head in your hand, it is gigantic. In contradiction to its powerful size, it has a mild and delicate flavour with sweet tones. Being truly huge, it is easy to peel, which is a plus when cooking the French recipe Chicken with 40 cloves of garlic (although 40 elephant cloves may be a little excessive – try 10). It has a flavoursome, light and mild sweet taste and is easy to digest. Like all garlic, it has so many suggested health-giving properties, from aiding athlete's foot, rheumatism and sore throats to insect bites and stings. What is certain is that it contains calcium, iron, potassium, thiamin, riboflavin, niacin and vitamin C.

Historically, garlic was recognized in the First World War for its antibiotic and bacterial properties. Even today, research is revealing that garlic may play an important part in controlling cholesterol, high blood pressure and heart disease. If stored in a cool place the perfect heads will stay fresh for months. If you can find some available during their summer season of August, buy a couple of heads and keep in a cool, dark place; alternatively they can be ordered via the internet all year round. Add to all recipes calling for garlic – although the number of cloves of garlic will need to be reduced if using elephant garlic.

recipe using elephant garlic, see page: 125

Allium tuberosum
Chinese chive

Chinese chives have been cultivated for centuries in Vietnam, Japan and China. These strong and pungent chives are also known as Chinese flowering leeks and in Arabic as *kurrat seeny*. Whether raw or cooked, they have a very powerful garlic aroma and flavour and are used extensively in *dim sum* and stir-fried and braised dishes. Almost all of the chive plant is eaten – the leaves, flower buds, flowers and stems. They can be found in most Asian markets and sold as either long green chive leaves (*gau choy*) or pale yellow flat leaves (*gau wong*). These two varieties are the same plant, but the yellow chives are grown under a chimney pot, devoid of light. These are considered a great Chinese delicacy. The flower-topped chives (*gau choy fa*) and a similar flower-headed chive (*gau choy sum*) are also available.

Chinese chives are found growing wild in China and grow tall slender leaves and tall flower heads, topped with greenish-white flowers that smell strongly of garlic. Use the yellow chives while very fresh and, like the green leaves, use chopped in dumplings, soups and stir-fries. In China and Japan the flowers are also ground and salted to make a savoury spice.

Keep all chives wrapped in a damp cloth at the bottom of the refrigerator for 1–2 days. Since the aroma is so strong, it is advisable to keep them in an airtight box to prevent all the other items in the refrigerator from smelling of garlic. They have similar medicinal properties as garlic and are believed to purify the blood. They contain vitamins A and C and trace minerals.

recipes using Chinese chives, see pages: 118; 130

Artocarpus heterophyllus
Jackfruit

This is a close relative of the breadfruit and, like its cousin, it grows to dramatic dimensions, up to 20 kg (44 lb) in weight. It originated in the rainforests of India and Malaysia and has since spread to Africa, throughout Asia, in particular Thailand, Vietnam, Indonesia and the Philippines, and across Polynesia, Australia and to tropical America.

Like the breadfruit, it grows from the low branches and trunk of a tree and can grow to a colossal size. The jackfruit is harvested from January to May and is often sold cut into sections, resembling wedges of pineapple, on market stalls or barrows that ply the streets of South-east Asia. It is really a collection of fruits fused together inside a hard, warted skin but is cooked and and used more often as a vegetable. The rough skin can form quite sharp warts and ripens from green to brown. It is used in both its unripe form and its sweeter more mature stage. When cut in half, it yields a yellow, creamy white or pink flesh surrounding many flat seeds. These seeds are also edible, and are often boiled and/or roasted like chestnuts. The flesh is fibrous and soft, with a pungent, almost durian-like aroma. It pulls apart into lobes of slightly sweet but otherwise bland, banana-flavoured flesh. It can be eaten raw but considering the size of each fruit it is also cooked while under-ripe and used in savoury main dishes. It is greatly improved by roasting or simmering in a curry sauce, in particular the lightly spiced curries of Indonesia like *Nasi campur* (a coconut milk, lime, green chilli and coriander sauce). In India it is eaten boiled, fried or raw and is also used in preserves. It has a carbohydrate-rich flesh containing vitamin C and potassium.

recipe using jackfruit, see page: 133

Blighia sapida
Ackee

As its Latin name suggests, *Blighia sapida* was named after Captain Bligh who took the ackee from Jamaica to Kew Gardens, England, in 1793. It is not indigenous to Jamaica but is derived from the West African akye fufo tree and is believed to have been taken to the West Indies on board a slave ship. The evergreen ackee tree survived the crossing and took to the climate and fertile soil of the Caribbean. Although it can be found on the other islands, it is in Jamaica that it grows the best and has become a major crop and everyday staple. It is cooked in curries with pigeon peas or with their other great favourite, dried salt fish. In fact ackee with salt fish is Jamaica's national dish. Ackee has a mild flavour that blends well with spices, their native Scotch bonnet chillies and other ingredients of Jamaican cooking. It is eaten for breakfast with eggs and in main dishes such as ackee patties.

Outside of the Caribbean, the yellow pulp is rarely seen in its fresh form. Harvested twice a year from January to March and then again from June to August, it is more commonly available canned. It is exported across the world to the overseas West Indian communities of Britain and North America. The main reason for canning the ackee pulp is that the pulp is the only part of the harvested fruit that is edible. Ackee grows on a large tree in oval pink pods which, when opened, contain black seeds covered by the characteristic fluffy yellow pulp. This pulp resembles large pieces of scrambled egg and needs to be carefully handled to prevent the ackee breaking up during cooking. The fleshy pulp is removed from the poisonous pink pod and canned ready for use.

It is rich in fatty acids, in particular linoleic acid, and is considered highly nutritious and vital to the fatty acid intake of the Jamaican population.

Its mild flavour works well in the pan with all fish. Toss in spices such as pepper, chillies and paprika and add to drained cans of beans and chopped tomatoes. Eat with plenty of rice.

recipe using ackee see pages: 131

Brassica rapa var. chinensis
Pak choi

Pak choi is older than Chinese cabbage and has been cultivated in China since the 5th century. It originally grew in southern China but is now cultivated across Asia, in particular Thailand, Hong Kong and Taiwan, but also in Europe and North America.

Part of the Cruciferae family, it has fleshy bright green leaves that are attached to thick, white fleshy stems. They look more like Swiss chard than a cabbage and the flavour is slightly peppery. The whole plant is edible – the stems and leaves, if the plant is allowed to mature it will flower and the flowers are edible too.

Pak choi is greatly favoured in all South-east Asian cooking and is quick to prepare and cook. In Korea it is greatly appreciated in the pickled cabbage condiment *kim chi*, and in China it is the ingredient in Chinese seaweed – not seaweed at all, but finely shredded and deep-fried pak choi.

Pak choi (also known as bok choy) is a fine vegetable that can take strong flavours, but is bright enough to be cooked on its own and stand up to attention on the table. The plants are usually cut when young before the buds form and flowers open. This vegetable is rich in calcium, iron and vitamin A.

There are many similar Chinese cabbages like choi sum (Chinese flowering cabbage), with its crisp and tender texture and a delicate flavour. All are ideal for stir-fries and other oriental dishes and are at their best late in the year.

recipe using pak choi, see page: 121

Capsicum annuum
Hot chilli peppers

There are two distinct sections to the pepper family – the sweet bell peppers and the hot peppers, better known as chillies. Chillies were used in Mexico 9000 years ago and began to be cultivated around 2000 years ago. They came to Asia from Central America and were quickly adopted throughout the Asian countries. Chillies vary greatly in their characteristics of colour and heat. The chillies used in Thailand, Indonesia, Malaysia and southern India are ragingly hot. The Indonesians pulp them into a sambal, which is used daily, and the Malaysians use them in their *rempah*, a similar sauce. Chillies are members of the deadly nightshade family and are rich in vitamins C, A and E. What all chillies have in common is capsaicin, the oily substance found in the ribs near to the seeds. Capsaicin gives chillies their heat and if the seeds are removed, the heat of the chilli is diminished. The growing conditions of the plant can affect the levels of capsaicin – the hotter the conditions, the hotter the chilli. As chillies are allowed to mature they become sweeter. There are many types of chilli, which vary in colour, size, shape and strength. The following are a small selection:

Anaheim – large, mild chillies used extensively in California. They are similar to Kashmiri chillies and are used fresh or dried. **Cayenne** – these are approximately 7.5 cm (3 inches) long, bright red and have a very hot flavour. They are used fresh or dried. **Jalapeño** – these plump chillies grow in Mexico and are about 5 cm (2 inches) long and bright green in colour. They are used pickled or fresh. **Kashmiri** – long, tapered chillies with a mild flavour, used in Indian cooking. They are used for their dark red colour and are normally found dried. **Serrano** – these green or red chillies are widely available. They are short and plump and about 4 cm (1½ inches) long. Their flavour is both hot and rich. **Bird** – intensely hot chillies used greatly in Thai cooking. They are no more than 2 cm (1 inch) long and can be red or green. **Togarashi** – these are tiny fiercely hot Japanese chillies which are grated with daikon radish as a condiment. **Scotch bonnet** – round and lantern-shaped chillies which can be red or yellow. They are fiercely hot and used in Jamaican cooking.

recipes using hot chilli peppers, see pages: 84; 88; 91; 92; 96; 100; 101; 109; 110; 118; 120; 121; 125; 126; 129; 130; 133; 134; 137; 138; 147; 168

Colocasia esculenta & Colocasia antiquorum

Eddoe & Taro

The eddoe and taro are very close cousins, both belonging to the Colocasia genus. It is a well-travelled family with a well-mapped history – both can trace their origins back to South-east Asia but today they are grown across the Pacific, in Africa and in the West Indies. The major difference between the two tubers is that the eddoe is tastier and smaller than the taro.

The taro is native to Indo-Malaysia and was brought with the Polynesians, by canoe, to Hawaii where the original indigenous tribe, the *Kanaka maoli*, used it as a primary source of food. These tubers were, and are still, considered 'a life-giving source' and 'soul food'. Both the root and large 'elephant's ear' leaves are used ritually during Hawaiian religious ceremonies.

The eddoe is found in Africa and the West Indies and is the classic ingredient in West Indian pepperpot stew. To add to the confusion over these vegetables, here the eddoe is also known as *malanga* while the taro is known as *dasheen*. The eddoe is thought to have travelled to the West Indies as an early export from China, as a cheap food for the West Indian slaves. In China it grows in the south and up to the far north and is harvested from August and September. In the West Indian islands of Trinidad and Tobago, however, it is harvested from October to May and is exported to Britain and Holland.

The rough, hairy tubers are peeled and cooked whole or sliced, baked, boiled, steamed and mashed. They have a sweet taste, if a little pungent, and are used in Chinese medicine to treat ulcers and psoriasis. The flesh is fibrous and can be white, yellow, greenish or pink. It is used in stewed chicken and pork dishes with Mediterranean influences, is added to soups and is also boiled and eaten with sugar. Both the eddoe and the taro are high in vitamins A, B and C, calcium, iron and carbohydrates and are 70 per cent starch protein. Most plants have edible leaves which are cooked as greens, like spinach. These leafy greens are very similar to spinach and are grown in the West Indies as callaloo. Callaloo soup is a speciality in Trinidad and the French Antilles.

recipe using eddoes, see page: 94

Bamboo shoot

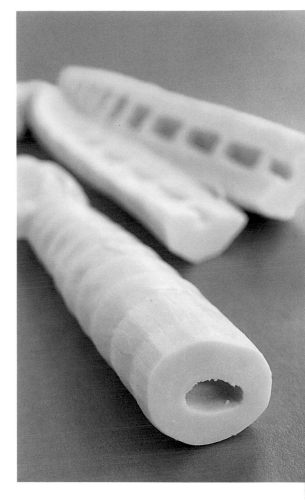

The bamboo shoot is the very young shoot of the fast-growing bamboo plant that has grown prolifically in China and South-east Asia for longer than anyone can remember. The young shoots grow into the long canes greatly used throughout Asia for all manner of purposes including cups, furniture and even scaffolding. Often referred to as 'miracle grass', it surprisingly belongs to the extended grass family.

Bamboo shoots are vital to Asian cooking, in particular Chinese and Vietnamese. The succulent flesh is greatly noted for its texture and flavour. The shoots are shredded or sliced and added to many dishes, from stir-fries and soups to Thai coconut curries, and are also finely chopped and used to fill spring rolls and stuffed wontons. Most of the bamboo shoots exported worldwide come from the huge plantations growing in Thailand, Taiwan and China, although Australia will probably be a contender in the future.

The bamboo shoots available in the Chinese spring are obviously younger and smaller than the stronger and more fibrous winter shoots and are far preferred for their delicacy. Dug out of the ground when the shoots are about 15 cm (6 inches) long, they are stripped of their green-yellow papery outer covering and boiled to make them edible. The smaller and younger they are, the softer and less fibrous the texture. Freshly boiled, they have a delicious crisp sweet flavour that cannot be equalled by canned varieties. Generally they are used in oriental cooking as an extender and absorb other flavours easily. Nutritionally they have the same properties as an onion and provide a good source of fibre. Unfortunately fresh bamboo shoots are not usually available in the West, unless you personally grow one of the ten edible types for yourself. Canned supplies are the norm and are available ready-shredded or sliced into oblongs. If possible, find a Chinese emporium and buy ready-cooked whole bamboo shoots that are often seen on display in large buckets. Select the bamboo shoot for yourself and cut and shred to your own specifications. Keep the bamboo shoot chilled and immersed in water until ready to use. They will keep this way for 4–5 days.

recipe using bamboo shoots, see page: 84

Dioscorea opposita
Yam

The yam is an ancient vegetable and has been a staple food since prehistoric times. These huge edible tubers are indigenous to Africa and Asia and are a vital accompaniment to the African Ivory Coast dish of *Foufou*.

They are greatly used in the West Indies where they are boiled, peppered and mashed and served alongside curries and stews as a filler, much like the common potato is used in Britain. Yams are high in starch, have quite a bland flavour and offer little nutritional content other than a good supply of fibre.

There are around ten types of yam from all over the tropics and they vary in size from medium to long tapered tubers with thick skins that look more like bark. The alata or winged yam is the most popular. The guinea yam (*Dioscorea rotundata*) is huge and is the yam most frequently used in the USA. It has yellow flesh and is also popular in West Africa and the West Indies.

The brown scaly skin has hair-like minor roots, like the casing on a brown coconut, and requires scrubbing and peeling before cooking. The flesh is dense and tends to be white, but can be yellow or purple. It has a much denser flesh than a potato and is far slower to cook. Because of the long slow cooking, yams are ideal in stews and slow-cooked soups. In general, yams are cooked by boiling and steaming but can also be chipped and roasted. Add extra flavour to yam mash by mixing it with other root vegetables like carrot or swede. Alternatively, add chopped parsley, coriander or spices such as fresh chilli or toasted ground coriander for an extra Jamaican flavour.

recipe using yams, see page: 141

Vigna sesquipedalis
Yard bean

The yard bean is thought to have originated in China but is also commercially grown in Vietnam, Thailand and Burma. It is closely related to the common dwarf bean, was introduced to America by the Spanish in the 16th century, and is grown to produce black-eyed peas. The yard bean plant is a climbing plant with large pale blue flowers and beans that earn their name by growing up to 30–90 cm (12–36 inches) in length. They are narrow, stringless beans which can be either pale or dark green and when cut in half have white, purple or black seeds at their centre.

The beans have a mild bean flavour and a crisp texture and are used in much the same way as French beans in Europe. Being so slim they cook quickly and can be stir-fried in a wok or eaten raw in dishes like the chilli-hot Thai salads that are lightly pounded with a pestle and mortar to tenderize the raw ingredients. Like the pea plant, the skin, leaves and shoots of the yard bean plant can all be eaten and are best steamed and then dressed with garlic olive oil.

Yard beans are also grown in India and China and are typically cooked in Canton in a black bean sauce or sautéed in a Szechwan sauce with pork, red pepper and soy sauce.

In the West they are available from spring through to summer. Choose bright green beans, which are firm and crisp if snapped in half. Often they can have blemish spots but as long as they are crisp do not be put off by these and use as normal beans. They contain vitamins A, C and F and some iron and trace elements.

recipes using yard beans, see pages: 100; 101   **61**

Eleocharis dulcis
Water chestnut

Water chestnuts are the corms (bulbs) of a perennial, reed-like plant with long hollow leaves that grows wild in shallow waters. The corms are the only edible part of the plant and develop under the water in the mud.

There are two types of chestnuts, the more common Chinese water chestnut and the water caltrop or horned chestnut, which is often sold alongside the water chestnut. The caltrop is easy to recognize with its distinctive pair of horns protruding from either side of the corms and tends to be beige while the water chestnut has a mahogany skin. The main difference between the two is that the water caltrop can only be eaten cooked and must be boiled for an hour to eliminate toxins.

Water chestnuts resemble chestnuts or small flower bulbs with their mahogany skin and tuft at the top of the nut. In China they grow them in rotation with rice in the paddy fields and the horse hoof-shaped corms are harvested when the outside skin has developed from pale beige to a rich brown. At this point they have reached their prime eating stage. They need to be peeled and can be eaten raw or lightly cooked in stir-fries.

If not peeled, they can be kept in the refrigerator for up to two weeks. They have a unique semi-sweet flavour and crisp flesh that is highly prized and used in Chinese, Thai and South-east Asian cooking. They are mostly used in savoury dishes but are also found in Asian desserts, served with palm fruits and brightly coloured iced drinks.

They are mostly found canned in the West, but during the winter months the whole corms can be found in Asian stores.

recipe using water chestnuts, see page: 122

Helianthus tuberosus & Stachys affinis sieboldii
Jerusalem & Chinese artichokes

The Jerusalem artichoke has been eaten since early Greek times when it was regarded as a great Mediterranean delicacy. These tubers were originally indigenous to North America and were brought to Europe in the 17th century. They are related to the globe artichoke and the majestic sunflower plant and are approximately 50 per cent carbohydrate. They have a sweet, dense flavour and are eaten both raw and cooked as an autumn vegetable but are also available through to the summer months. Scrub well but do not peel. Boil the tubers, sliced or quartered, for about 15 minutes or serve as they are, then sauté, roast or dip them in batter and deep-fry.

Chinese artichokes, also known as Crosnes, are not related to the Jerusalem artichoke, but are also tubers. They are natives of northern China and Japan and were brought to Paris in 1880 by an avid plant collector. The alternative name of Crosnes is in dedication to the French town of the same name, in which the returning collector planted his cache. From there they were introduced to Europe and became a great delicacy but have also remained quite rare, so expect to pay a price for them. The tubers come from a perennial plant and are often described as looking like maggots. The tiny, creamy white tubers are about the size of a small hazelnut and are made up of a series of round sections. They have a nutty flavour and are at their best when cooked simply. Scrub well before using and cook lightly by steaming, stir-frying or sautéing. Serve in a simple butter or olive oil dressing.

recipe using Jerusalem or Chinese artichokes, see page: 87

Hibiscus esculentis
Okra

Okra is related to the hibiscus flower and both are members of the mallow (*Malvaceae*) family. The edible pods are frequently known by the name ladies' fingers, after their shape and size, and gumbo, the southern dish they help to create. Natives of tropical Africa, they still grow wild in Ethiopia and Sudan and are also grown in Egypt and Asia, in particular India where they are called *bhindi*. From its native Africa, okra travelled south-west to Central America and arrived in Brazil around 1650. From there it was introduced to Europe and in particular the Mediterranean and the Balkans. The plants reached North America via the slave trade. The African Bantu tribes took a supply on board their slave boats and brought gumbo to the bosom of deep southern cooking. They are well used in Texan and the distinctive Cajun cooking of New Orleans and Louisiana.

Okra is harvested while young from the shrubby plant. The pods can be red, green, purple or white. Okra flowers only open for a day and then the pods quickly develop within a matter of 4–10 days. They are quickly harvested and exported worldwide. This vegetable does not store well and doesn't like being chilled, so store carefully.

The fuzzy green pods are approximately 5–10 cm (2–4 inches) long, and contain many seeds and a sticky mucilaginous juice that is used as a thickener in stews and gumbo and forms the secret ingredient in some well-known ketchups that don't roll from the jar without a good shake.

Okra contains plenty of calcium, magnesium, potassium and phosphorus, plus vitamin C, carotene and some of the B vitamins. When quickly fried, these nutrients are not greatly diminished so stir-fry, briefly boil, steam, bake or grill for 5–10 minutes.

recipes using okra, see pages: 96; 120

Ipomoea batatas
Sweet potato

Sweet potatoes are tuberous roots like a common potato but have a much longer shape and a denser flesh. They are distant relations of the common potato but unlike the common potato they like warmth and grow well in Asian and tropical South American countries. In general, sweet potatoes have a dense, dry flesh, which will require much more cooking than a standard potato.

There are two basic varieties of sweet potato, both of which have reddish skins. One has a sweeter orange-red flesh and the other a pale white flesh. The orange-red fleshed sweet potato, generally known as a yam in America but not actually related to the yam plant, is native to Asia but was found by Europeans in Central America in the 18th century. It has a sweet, deep orange flesh, which is highly regarded as good for roasting, boiling, frying and mashing.

The white sweet potato is smaller with a drier, slightly yellow flesh. It is not as rich but is certainly denser and requires longer cooking. Both types are used in savoury and sweet dishes, including Creole puddings and American autumn and winter recipes, sweet potato and apple pie being a particular favourite. They are particularly good cooked with apple and served with home-cooked ham and gammon joints. They are an important carbohydrate-rich food, and also contain some protein and sugar.

recipe using sweet potatoes, see page: 126

Ipomoea reptans aquatica
Morning glory (Swamp cabbage)

Morning glory is the green-leaved vegetable greatly used by the Thais, Vietnamese and Chinese. It is part of the Convolvulaceae family which also includes sweet potatoes, and is not actually a cabbage or a spinach plant, even though the leaves look very similar and are used in much the same way. It probably originated in Africa, but is now grown throughout South-east Asia and Australia. In the wild it grows rampantly in ditches and ponds and scrambles across banks on fish farms. It is an aquatic plant and is available all year round in a variety of forms including purple-stemmed varieties with narrow triangular leaves and white-stemmed varieties with wider leaves. It has characteristic hollow stems that are roughly chopped and cooked with the leaves. In Indonesia it is greatly used in Gado gado salad and in Thailand it is known as *Pak bung*. It is the main ingredient in the market stall dish *Pak bung fadang*, an everyday vegetable dish available in restaurants and markets across the country. It is also known by its alternative names of swamp cabbage and water spinach.

It has a very delicate, fresh flavour and can be quickly fried with garlic and chilli and served like spinach. The leaves cook quickly but the hollow stems retain their crisp texture and characteristic crunch. Morning glory is a vital ingredient in the Philippino dish of *Sinigang* – a sour fish stew. It can be found in many Asian stores that specialize in Thai and Malaysian ingredients. Buy very fresh and keep in the bottom of the refrigerator in a plastic bag for 1–2 days. It is rich in iron, calcium and vitamins A and C.

recipes using morning glory (swamp cabbage), see pages: 90; 118

Lagenaria siceraria
Dudhi

Dudhi or doodhi, depending on how you wish to spell it, is also known as bottle gourd. Part of the extensive gourd family, it has been used for thousands of years in the tropics and sub-tropics and is greatly represented in ancient Chinese art. However, it probably originated in southern Central America. It is known to have been in Mexico around 7000–5500 BC and has also been found in Egyptian tombs dating back to 3500–3300 BC. In the Middle East and South America the gourds are often left to dry out and their woody hard shells are used as bottles and drinking vessels. More often they are used young and fresh, when their unobtrusive flavour is added to soups and stews, as they mature their bitter flavour increases.

The dudhi grows on a climbing plant and has either a light or dark green skin. They can grow up to 1 m (3 feet) long and vary in shape from crooked neck, bottle-shaped, tapered to round. They are long and slightly bulbous at one end, with a smooth green skin. The rounded end contains seeds which can be scooped out to leave the edible, firm, white flesh. Dudhi can be found in Indian and West Indian shops and these days in some large supermarkets where the local community contains a mix of cultures. Peel, chop and discard any large seeds and, if young, boil in a little water like a marrow, simmer in vegetable dishes or sauté with delicate spices and herbs. The flesh is delicate and tastes a little like courgette. It does not have an important nutrient content, just small amounts of calcium, potassium and some vitamin C.

recipe using dudhi, see page: 114   **67**

Manihot esculenta
Cassava

Cassava root or tapioca, as it is known in Asia, is one of the most popular starch tubers grown throughout Africa, Central and South America and Asia. A native plant of South America, in particular Brazil and Colombia, it is as much part of the basic diet of present-day Brazilians as it was for the original Indian population. When the colonizing Portuguese arrived in Brazil in the 16th century, the main staple of the tribes of tropical South America was cassava (or tapioca as the Indians called it). From there it spread to Colombia, Panama and the West Indies.

It is used in much the same way as the European potato to create a carbohydrate-rich meal. In Indonesia the leaves are also consumed, cooked like spinach and eaten as a vegetable side dish. The leaves have a slightly bitter taste and, like spinach, a strong flavour. However, the tubers can vary from sweet to bitter tasting. The toxic bitter variety is extensively cultivated and processed into tapioca flakes, pearls or coarse flour. The tuber can't be eaten raw because of its poisonous, milky acrid juices but once washed, processed and dried, it forms tapioca, of school pudding fame. It is this cassava flour (*farinha de mandioca*) that is used extensively as a thickener in soups and stews and cooked as a cassava meal and browned in butter to accompany the Brazilian national dish, *Feijoada* – a stew of black beans, smoked meat and sausages. It is also baked into *Pao de queijo* – cheese rolls – and other breads and cakes.

The non-poisonous tubers of the sweeter cassava can be eaten without any processing as a simple vegetable. They are peeled, boiled and eaten like potatoes. They are not dissimilar to a potato or yam and are mashed, chipped and fried or boiled and used in many types of sweet and savoury dishes like the Brazilian *Farofa de manteiga*, a scrambled egg dish with onion, parsley and cassava.

On the outside the tubers have a rough brown and hairy skin, while inside the flesh is bright and white. Peel the tuber, cut up the flesh and boil until soft enough to mash. Alternatively, grate or thinly slice the flesh and then boil it or use in other vegetable dishes. Like the potato, the tuber is almost all starch with a few trace elements of minerals such as calcium.

Momordica charantia
Karela

These bitter gourds are closely related to the smooth-skinned European cucumber – both are part of the Cucurbitaceae family. In fact, karela look very similar to a small ridged cucumber but, as its other name of bitter gourd suggests, the flesh of these vegetables is very bitter and needs to be prepared well in advance of cooking.

It is an ancient climbing plant, cultivated for thousands of years across the tropics and sub-tropics and is also found in China. It is believed to have originated in India and has travelled with the overseas Indians to Britain and some parts of Africa and Singapore. In the centre of the flesh are many seeds which are discarded before cooking. Karela tastes best when sliced and soaked for an hour in salt water to remove the bitterness. They are hugely important in both Chinese and Indian cooking and are braised or steamed, made into soups, used in *dim sum*, or stuffed with pork and cooked with Indian spices.

Usually they are sold at the unripe, green stage. The smaller they are, the less bitter they are and they should be chosen when firm and unblemished. As the skin ripens to yellow, orange and sometimes white, it loses flavour and develops a strange texture. The Chinese and Indians consider them to have strong medicinal properties and use them to reduce blood sugar levels and control diabetes. They have blood-purifying properties and are used to cool the body. They also contain essential amino acids, are high in dietary fibre and potassium and contain some calcium, iron and zinc. If allowed to ripen they also contain vitamin C and folic acid. Most interestingly, proteolipin – a naturally occurring substance that strengthens the immune system – has been identified in these vegetables and is being developed as an anti-cancer agent.

recipe using karela, see page: 116   **69**

Moringa oleifera
Drumstick

The drumstick tree is a native of the sub-Himalayan regions of north-west India and Bangladesh and also grows in Africa, Arabia, South-east Asia, through the Pacific, Caribbean and South America.

The plant is known as both the drumstick tree and also the horseradish tree, since the colonizing Europeans grated the root into a condiment similar to, and substituted for, horseradish. Much later this condiment was found to be toxic with fatal possibilities, so it is no longer eaten. The leaves of the tree are also consumed for their rich sources of vitamins A, B and C, calcium, iron and protein, and the fragrant flowers are gathered, dipped in batter and fried. However, it is the long bean-like pods that are the most valued part of this plant.

The pods are at first a light green colour and are slim and tender. As they grow more mature the outside dries to a lightly wooded papery shell and becomes deep green. While young they are used in a similar way to European beans, but as they grow older the fleshy pulp and round or triangular seeds at the centre become the main attraction and are used in soups and stews. By the time they have been harvested and flown to the other side of the world, many drumsticks resemble their namesakes. However, the tough exterior hides the delicious asparagus- or marrow-flavoured pulp and delicate seeds. Trimmed and cut into sections, they are cooked for an hour in a soup or stew. They are then slit open and the flesh and seeds are scooped out into the dish. They are considered a good source of calcium and vitamins and contain a high percentage of amino acids.

recipe using drumsticks, see page: 140

Musa paradisiaca
Plantain

The plantain is very like its cousin the dessert banana except that it is larger and only eaten when cooked. The plantain is slightly curved, with green, brown, yellow or red skin and lots of brown scars. Unlike the banana that grows wild throughout Asia, plantains originated in Central America and have become a staple for the people of South America, the West Indies and tropical Africa.

The plantain plant grows from underground rhizomes and has huge leaves and seedless fruits, which develop without pollination from unisex flowers. They are generally straighter than bananas and can't be kept in the refrigerator. They are used both ripe and unripe. When the skin is peeled away, it reveals a fibrous and much less sweet fruit that softens and improves with cooking. It is primarily used as a cooked vegetable with West Indian stews and curries and is also added sliced to cakes and puddings. It is one of the major ingredients in the Jamaican jerk sauce which is used to marinate goat, chicken or any other meat. This is a thick, highly spiced mixture that penetrates the meat which is then cooked over a barbecue. Spicy and delicious, it is perfect served with very thinly sliced and fried plantain chips.

Plantains are rich in carbohydrates with some calcium, vitamin A and B. Do not be put off by the dark markings on the skins. Hold them in the hand; they should be heavy and slightly firm. If they are very soft and squashy, avoid them.

recipe using plaintains, see page: 96

Musa sapientum
Banana flower

This is the majestic flower of the banana plant. Banana flowers are large, pointed heads of many petals, either pink or yellow in colour. They are similar in appearance to candle-shaped magnolia flowers. If you peel back each of the petal-like scales, underneath you can see the very immature bananas. They almost look like stamens at this stage. With time as the flower develops and grows along its central stalk, each petal falls off and leaves the hands of bananas to grow from the stem, while the developing flower stays perched at the very end of the clusters of bananas. As much as the flower heads are vital for the growth of new bananas, they are also edible and considered a delicacy. In countries across Asia, from Burma to Indonesia, the flower head is shredded and eaten in salad-style mixtures. In Thailand the heads are gently boiled and served with the northern Shan-style chilli-hot *Nam prik ong*. They are added to the Philippine *Linabog*, a coconut curry with dried fish, and in, Laos they are served as part of the national dish of *Khao phoume*. The flavour is mild and most similar to an artichoke or fresh bamboo shoot. To cook, plunge the flower head into boiling water for 20 minutes. Discard the outer petals and eat the inside petals as you would an artichoke, sucking on the base of the leaves and stripping the flesh from the bases. Otherwise cook the shredded flower in coconut-laced curries or mix with ingredients like spring onions, bean sprouts, coriander leaves and tomatoes. Banana flowers can be found in the West in Thai supermarkets or other Asian stores. They are well worth asking for, or even ordering. If you live in a warm, sheltered area try growing your own, making sure to protect them from frost with layers of hessian and a chimney pot. It's worth a go – but the plants will take seven years to reach flowering size.

recipes using banana flower, see pages: 100; 133

Nelumbium nuciferum
Lotus

This is a highly sacred plant grown since
ancient times throughout China and India
and now used extensively across the Far
East. It belongs to the Nymphaeacea family
and is a perennial waterlily that grows in
terraced paddy fields and shallow ponds.
The lotus plant and flower have always
been considered auspicious and symbolize
Buddhist beliefs in peace and harmony.
They are also believed by the Chinese to
symbolize the birth of male offspring. The
large, waxy leaves that distinctively curl at
the edges, the buds, the seeds and the root
are all edible. The fresh roots are a series
of bulbous sections separated by narrow
necks that make them look like a string of
dark sausages. Although lotus root is
mostly available canned, it can be found
fresh in Asian stores. Peel the outer
coating, slice the flesh and immediately
drop into water mixed with lemon juice or
vinegar. If left out in the air, the flesh will
turn brown, like an apple. They have a
distinctive crisp texture and mild, nutty
artichoke flavour, similar to water chestnuts.

The leaves are added raw to salads or
used as wrappers for fish or meat before
roasting or steaming. The food will absorb some of their flavour, aroma and greenish colour.
Sometimes the leaves are available in a dried form and need to be soaked before wrapping.
The lotus roots are ochre coloured and look like a dented potato. When cut, they reveal a
honeycomb structure of perforated channels. The slices have a flower pattern which is
greatly used for its artistic contribution to Chinese and Japanese banquet dishes. In India it
is often boiled and mashed and added to fritters and vegetable dishes. In China it is also
grown for its astringent medicinal properties believed to be good for depression and also
lung and intestinal ailments. Nutritionally they are very good. The root is rich in starch,
vitamin B and C while the seeds, which are eaten as a snack or pounded into a pulp and
used in desserts, are rich in fat, protein and starch.

Psophocarpus tetragonolobus
Winged bean

Winged beans grow on a perennial climbing plant and are often referred to as magic beans. They have edible flowers, pods and tubers and provide a good source of protein and oil. Each bean has four corners and is either rectangular or square in shape with a frilly edge running along each side. When the beans are cut in half, the frilly edge makes them appear to have wings – hence the name. The winged bean is believed to have originated in South-east Asia and is also known as the asparagus bean or goa bean. They were found in the Molucca islands in Indonesia but are also thought to be natives of Madagascar and Africa.

Highly regarded in the Far East for their mild flavour and crisp texture, they are now commercially grown right across Asia from India to New Guinea.

The bean pods hang in clusters from a high bush and are harvested when the pods are bright green and not much more than 7.5 cm (3 inches) in length. The pods are shiny and have round red beans in the centre. They are a highly nutritious vegetable and are treated, used and eaten like green beans. Virtually all of the plant is edible – the bean-like pods, the young shoots and blue flowers. Eat raw, blanched or added to vegetable dishes or salads. In Thailand the beans are chopped up and used in a salad called *Tua poo*, while in Burma the roots and seeds are cooked, mashed and served with curries. If cooking, steam or parboil for only a few minutes to retain the texture and flavour or slice and stir-fry with garlic and chilli or black beans. Buy winged beans while they are young and crisp and keep in the refrigerator for up to one week.

Raphanus sativus
Daikon

This great white radish is vital to Chinese and Japanese cooking but is said to have originated in the Mediterranean and was taken to China around 500 BC. The large, tapered radish has a very hot mustard flavour and crisp, watery flesh. It has a thin, smooth skin and looks very much like a large white carrot. It varies greatly in size from 5–100 cm (2–40 inches).

There are Chinese and Japanese varieties, both of which are summer radishes and akin to the small red European varieties. They are used extensively in South-east Asia for their distinctive flavour and texture, in particular in Japan. There the radish is believed to have strong medicinal powers for alleviating fever, sore throats and colds.

It has a flavour similar to horseradish and is often served alongside the Japanese wasabi, a very hot horseradish-like plant that gives a kick to sushi. In India it is known as mooli and is eaten both raw and cooked. There is also a black-skinned Spanish radish, which is very similar apart from its skin and a red skinned variety. All are known for their high vitamin C content and are highly favoured for their digestive properties.

Buy when the radishes are young and of medium size. The larger they grow, the more fibrous the texture. They are always eaten during the Oriental New Year and are used in Japan as a condiment and also as a marinade for tenderizing octopus and to remove strong odours from oily fish. Look for radishes that are free of cracks and are firm and crisp. To retain their crisp texture and prevent water loss, keep them wrapped at the bottom of the refrigerator.

recipe using daikon, see page: 102

Saccharum officinarum
Sugar cane

Sugar cane is part of the Poaceae family and grows like a perennial grass – very tall and stout. Like bamboo, the sugar cane plant can grow to 5 m (15 ft) with solid yellow-green canes. It is grown commercially in China, Vietnam, the East Indies, Hawaii and South America and many other tropical and sub-tropical countries. The sugar cane is crushed and the sugary juices that are extracted from the canes are then boiled down into raw unrefined sugar. They are then refined into everyday sugars like granulated, caster and icing sugars. Sugar is a very rich commodity for worldwide trade and has a high commercial value. It is of great value to all types of cooking and in particular to the Asian and West Indian countries where the heat of chilli is cooled and counteracted by the sweetness of sugar. It is a well-known fact that to quell the heat of a very hot curry it is much better to drink a highly sweet carbonated drink than water.

In Asia sugar comes from three sources: sugar cane, sugar palm and the coconut palm but it is the sugar cane that has the greatest use. The canes are crushed through a roadside mangle to extract the sweet juice that is drunk on every street corner and in market places by adults and children alike. South-east Asian children also love to chew on the sticks of

sugar cane and suck out the raw sugar juice from the fibrous matter – rather like a fruit snack. Strong teeth are required to pull back the bark, but the high sugar content has a devastating effect on the health of their teeth. In Vietnam the sugar cane is also utilized as a cooking ingredient by cutting it into kebab sticks upon which a prawn paste is moulded and grilled. Sugar cane has little nutritious content – it is obviously high in energy and calories from the raw sugar, but also contains iron.

recipe using sugar cane, see page: 92

Sechium edule
Chayote

Chayotes can often be seen in Chinatown where their crisp, bright green skin and slight pear shape might make you believe it belongs to the fruit bowl. It is, in fact, part of the squash family and originates in Central America and although sometimes used in South American desserts, it is mostly used as a vegetable. It is commercially grown all year round in Australia, the deep south of America, Mexico, Guatemala and the West Indies on a climbing vine that fruits abundantly.

Chayotes are also known as cho-cho, or vegetable pear, and are known to have been grown and eaten by the Aztecs. They have a high water content and the bigger the vegetable grows the more dilute the flavour becomes, so choose small vegetables. Chayotes need to be cooked like a potato before eating and are used in much the same way as other squashes. The texture and mild flavour is rather like a pumpkin and they can also be braised as a vegetable or cooked to make a chutney.

The fruit pod is about 12 cm (5 in) long and tapers like a pear, the skin is pale green and the flesh is a pale green pulp with a large seed in the centre. When stuffing it, first cook the chayote whole in boiling water until tender. Cut off the top of the chayote and scoop out the seed and the flesh to make a cavity. A favourite method is to stuff the centre with a vegetable or mildly spiced lamb mixture and slowly bake until tender. Otherwise slice the vegetable, discarding the seed, and use in vegetable curries or braise with beef or lamb in casseroles. These vegetables also make good fritters served with a spicy sauce.

Solanum andigenum
South American blue potato

The South American, or Peruvian, blue potato, like all other members of the potato family, is a native of Peru and was cultivated in South America 6000 years ago in the areas surrounding Lake Titicaca. Since then the potato has been one of the main food sources for the local Inca people and also for Europeans who have become hooked on the tubers.

Around 1550, the Spanish introduced the potato to Europe. It first came to England with Sir Walter Raleigh in 1586, but surprisingly it remained unknown in North America until the 18th century when Irish settlers took the tubers with them to the new lands of America. The potato was in use in London from 1590 and fast became a major crop, taking to the cold British climate.

The potato will root where cereal crops find it hard to grow, which is why it grows so well in the diverse Andean landscape. The potato is the world's fourth largest crop after rice, wheat and corn. Globally potatoes provide more food per year than the total production of fish and meat. They are virtually fat free and contain vitamins C and B. The blue potatoes also contain minerals which cause their bright blue colouring.

There are over 4000 varieties of potato, of which the blue potatoes are among the most rare and exotic. The South American blue potatoes are farmed from Argentina to Paraguay and are also cultivated in North America. They have an unusual vibrant blue to purple

pigmentation with a dense, sweet flesh and a slight nutty flavour.

Another variety of blue potato, the blue Congo potato, grows on the west coast of Finland and has a firm texture and a subtle flavour. They have a rather unusual bright violet-purple flesh with a texture not dissimilar to a waxy new potato and a sweet flavour similar to a King Edward. In Finland they are served at royal banquets and are considered a great delicacy. They are harvested from September to October and are available throughout the winter months. In Finland they are boiled and served like new potatoes, or mashed with cream or yogurt.

Also available are: a baking potato called All Blue which is best served roasted or steamed to retain its colour; Lavendar, named after its lavender flesh and skin; and Blue Cloud, a light purple potato with white marbling. Steam blue potatoes, bake them, mash them or microwave, but avoid boiling them in order to retain their flavour and prevent the colour leaching out.

recipe using South American blue potatoes (Congo potatoes), see page: 112

Solanum melongena & Solanum undatum
Pea & white egg aubergines

Aubergines, or eggplants, are available
all year round in one of their various
shapes and colours. Along with the
common potato, they are members of the
Solanaceae family and are believed to have
originated in India, where they have been
cultivated for over 4000 years. The fruits
can be white, purple or green and vary
greatly in shape and size, from pea-sized,
to oval egg and much larger. The name
eggplant obviously arises from the similarity
that the white versions have with the
humble egg.

They travelled from the Middle East to
southern Europe with the Moors and have
become a vital ingredient in Mediterranean
cooking, in particular in Greece where
Moussaka wouldn't be what it is without
the aubergine and in Turkey where *Imam
bayildi*, an aubergine purée, is one of the
national dishes.

The most popular aubergine in India is the
dark purple, elongated fruit, known as *brinjal*, while in Szechwan, Laos, Cambodia and
Thailand the hard round green or white globes are favoured. In Japan the aubergines are
smaller and slender and greatly prized in tempura, while the tiny pea aubergines are used
primarily in Thailand where they grow in clusters like green peas on a series of branches.
They have a bitter flavour, are very crisp and are added whole to curries and soups. The
Philippine talong eggplant is long and slender and a royal purple colour. It has more flavour
than large European varieties and its name translates as 'Malaysian purple melon'.

Generally aubergines have a bland, porous flesh which is pithy and full of small seeds.
They should be chosen when firm to the touch and brightly coloured. Tap the pod and it
should sound hollow, but if you press the flesh and an indentation is left, it is not at its
best. Keep aubergines cool in the refrigerator and they will last for 2–3 weeks. During
preparation, they discolour quickly and should be cut just before cooking. Many people
recommend salting the European oval purple aubergine to remove the water and bitter
juices, but this is not necessary. If you do want to do this, put the chopped aubergine in a
colander, sprinkle well with salt and press with a plate and a heavy weight. When the juices
have run out of the flesh, rinse the salt off the pieces and drain well before cooking.

Aubergines are rich in vitamin C and all the B vitamins, with small amounts of iron and
calcium. Most of the nutrients are located in the skin and not in the flesh.

recipes using aubergines, see pages: 116; 125; 137; 140

Salsify Tragopogon porrifolius

Salsify is a long tapered root, which is brown and muddy. It was much prized in Victorian times and was used in soups and salads and cooked as a vegetable, but recently it has been much overlooked. Also known as the oyster plant, salsify is a long gnarled root of the daisy family. It is thought to have a vague flavour of oysters, thus the name, and has a close cousin called scorzonera, which is almost identical in texture and flavour but has a black skin. When young, both plants have edible leaves that can be eaten in salads or cooked like spinach. Salsify skin is white, but both roots have a crisp, white flesh. It is a native of Europe and the Mediterranean and has been used greatly since the 17th century, both as a vegetable and also for its medicinal properties, to treat heartburn and liver complaints.

Salsify is available from October to March and can be kept unwashed in the bottom of the refrigerator, stored in a plastic bag, for about a week. Use boiled and grated or boiled then griddled. First scrape the roots to remove the skin, cut into slices, batons or sections and drop into water with added lemon juice or vinegar to prevent the flesh browning due to oxidation. Some suggest boiling the roots with the skin on for about 10 minutes and then rinsing under running cold water. This way the salsify sheds its skin like a snake.

Salsify is 8–10 per cent carbohydrate and is a good source of protein, fibre, calcium and sodium. When cooked it has a slightly glossy appearance.

recipe using salsify, see page: 115

Coccinia grandis
Tindori

Tindori are also known as ivy gourds or gentleman's toes – the latter, one assumes, refers to their size and shape. They are also known by their other Indian names of tindola and pawal. Tindori are native to India and are a highly prized vegetable, for both their culinary and medicinal properties. They are sold by the barrel in markets and from roadside stalls. They are tender little vegetables, green in colour, with long white longitudinal stripes on all sides. As they ripen, some varieties can develop a red colour and a slight bitter flavour. Tindori are part of the squash family, but unlike their large cousins, this tiny squash only grows to the size of a large gooseberry. In fact they look more like small, oval gherkins or stunted mini cucumbers.

In India they are used in everyday vegetable curries or are cooked as a basic vegetable to accompany many other dishes. Some varieties have a bitter flavour, but since they easily absorb the flavours of spices and herbs, this bitter flavour is often masked. Prepare them by slicing thinly and then lightly frying in vegetable oil with a variety of toasted spices. Serve alongside daal and chapatis for a quick meal or with tandoori chicken or lamb with pilau rice.

Choose tindori that are bright green, firm and crisp. Rinse well, slice and cook as preferred. It is best to lightly cook them to retain some of their crisp texture, or to eat them raw and thinly sliced in salad or raita mixtures.

recipes using tindori, see pages: 138

recipe section

84–173

1 medium cooked crab

1 tablespoon lime juice

50 g (2 oz) thin rice noodles

125 g (4 oz) bamboo shoots

4 spring onions

10 mint sprigs

small bunch of coriander

12 rice paper wrappers

salt and pepper

Dipping sauce

2 tablespoons Thai fish sauce

2 teaspoons sesame oil

1 tablespoon rice or white wine vinegar

1 teaspoon caster sugar

1 small red chilli, chopped

6 coriander leaves, torn

1 tablespoon roasted peanuts, chopped

To serve

lime wedges

red chillies

mint sprigs

Serves 4

Fresh spring rolls make a great start to a meal or a fun appetizer at drinks parties or buffets. Make them as late as possible and keep the plate covered with clear film to stop the rice paper wrappers from drying out. Crab can be substituted with prawns, strips of seared beef or with avocado, cucumber or tomato. The wrappers can be found in Asian stores. When dry they are very brittle and look like plastic. Soak briefly in warm water and they become supple. Do not over-soak or they will break when you are trying to roll them up.

1. To make the dipping sauce, put the fish sauce, sesame oil, vinegar, sugar and chilli in a small saucepan and heat gently to dissolve the sugar. Remove from the heat and cool. When cold add the coriander and peanuts.

2. Break open the crab, discard the stomach sack and dead man's fingers, remove all the white and brown meat and mix together. Add the lime juice, season to taste with salt and pepper and mix well to combine.

3. Put the rice noodles in a large bowl, cover with boiling water and leave to stand for 4 minutes to allow the noodles to soften and swell. Drain well and rinse in cold water.

4. Cut the bamboo shoots and spring onions into thin julienne strips. Remove the mint and coriander leaves from the stalks. Now the filling ingredients are ready.

5. Dip each of the rice paper wrappers in warm water for 1 minute to soften. Shake off the excess water and lay on a work surface. Put a little of the crabmeat on one side of the circle, top with strips of bamboo and spring onions, rice noodles, and then add a few mint and coriander leaves.

6. Fold the bottom edge of the wrapper over the ends of the filling and then roll the crabmeat end over and continue to roll to create a cigar shape. Put on a plate, cover and repeat until you have twelve plump rolls. Pour the dipping sauce into small bowls and serve alongside the fresh rolls, with lime wedges, chillies and mint sprigs.

fruit & vegetable information: bamboo shoot page 59; chillies page 57

bamboo, coriander
& crab fresh rolls

californian
hand rolls

These hand rolls can be served ready rolled or with all the ingredients laid out on a plate for the guests to make up as the meal progresses. Add freshly cooked prawns or squid to make the rolls even tastier.

175 g (6 oz) sushi rice

350 ml (12 fl oz) cold water

2 tablespoons rice wine vinegar

2 teaspoons caster sugar

1 tablespoon toasted sesame seeds

8 small square nori seaweed sheets

1 avocado, peeled and thickly sliced

7 cm (3 in) piece cucumber, cut into strips

handful of watercress or mustard cress

3 tablespoons salmon eggs

chives

To serve

pickled ginger

wasabi

soy sauce

Serves 4

1. Wash the rice in a sieve under cold running water for 2 minutes. Put the rice in a large saucepan and just cover with the cold water. Bring to the boil, cover the pan and reduce the heat to a simmer. Cook for 20 minutes or until the moisture has been absorbed.

2. Put the vinegar and sugar in a small pan and heat gently to dissolve the sugar. Remove from the heat and allow to cool. Remove the rice from the heat and leave covered for 10 minutes. Fluff with a fork and sprinkle with the sugar and vinegar mix. Turn out on to a tray or baking sheet and leave to cool, turning occasionally.

3. When the rice has cooled, sprinkle with the sesame seeds. Take a sheet of seaweed and place a tablespoon of cooled rice to one side. Top with a slice of avocado, some strips of cucumber and watercress, then roll into a cone. Dampen the edge of the seaweed with water and secure the roll.

4. Arrange the salmon eggs and chives in the tops of the rolls. Serve with a side dish of pickled ginger and a dish of wasabi and soy sauce mixed together, in which to dip the rolls just before eating.

fruit & vegetable information: nori seaweed (sea vegetables) page 51

roasted chinese
artichoke soup

375 g (12 oz) **Jerusalem or Chinese artichokes**

25 g (1 oz) **melted butter**

1 **onion, finely chopped**

1 **tablespoon olive oil**

1 **thyme sprig**

600 ml (1 pint) **vegetable or chicken stock**

150 ml (¼ pint) **double cream**

salt and pepper

thick bread croûtons, to serve

Salsa dulce

1 **garlic clove**

25 g (1 oz) **dry breadcrumbs**

1 **tablespoon chopped flat leaf parsley**

1 **tablespoon chopped dill**

1 **tablespoon chopped tarragon**

1 **small red pepper, deseeded and finely chopped**

3 **tablespoons olive oil**

Serves 4

Chinese or Jerusalem artichokes can be used in this soup. The gentle roasting of the artichokes contributes a slightly smoky flavour to the soup while the salsa dulce, *made with green herbs and sweet red pepper, adds a dash of colour and a punch of aroma. Serve steaming hot in big bowls; add the thick croûtons just before you take the soup to the table.*

1. Scrub the artichokes to remove any earth and cut the Jerusalem artichokes in half if they are large. Put in a small baking tin and drizzle the melted butter over the top. Sprinkle with salt and pepper and cook in the centre of a preheated oven at 200°C (400°F), Gas Mark 6 for 30 minutes or 10 minutes for Chinese artichokes, or until cooked through and lightly browned.

2. Lightly fry the chopped onion in the oil until wilted and then add the roasted artichokes, thyme leaves and stock and bring to a gentle boil. Reduce the heat and simmer for 10 minutes.

3. Make the salsa by combining the garlic, breadcrumbs, parsley, dill and tarragon in a food processor or blender. When mixed and finely chopped, add the red pepper and olive oil. Season to taste with salt and pepper and mix to a coarse purée.

4. When the soup is cooked, remove from the heat and purée in a food processor or blender until smooth. Alternatively, pass through a fine sieve. Return to the pan and reheat gently. When hot, season to taste with salt and pepper and add the cream.

5. Serve the soup piping hot, top each serving with a thick croûton and a spoonful of salsa. Just before eating, stir the salsa into the soup.

fruit & vegetable information: Jerusalem & Chinese artichokes page 63

4 tablespoons vegetable oil

250 g (8 oz) firm tofu, cut into cubes

1.2 litres (2 pints) vegetable stock

1 tablespoon rice wine vinegar

1 tablespoon mirin or dry sherry

1 sweet white onion, sliced

250 g (8 oz) raw udon or
egg noodles

125 g (4 oz) bean sprouts

1 red chilli, finely sliced

4 spring onions, finely sliced

50 g (2 oz) enoki or
shiitake mushrooms

1 tablespoon fried garlic

handful of coriander leaves

2 tablespoons miso (optional)

4 kaffir lime leaves, shredded

To serve

soy sauce

crushed chilli flakes

Serves 4

These big-bowl Japanese soups contain just about everything for one meal. Tofu is a favourite in the East and pairs well with the other oriental ingredients. It can, however, be replaced with prawns or grilled chicken fillets. The strange-looking enoki mushrooms are available in large supermarkets, but if they prove too difficult to find, use either fresh shiitake mushrooms or dried mushrooms soaked for 30 minutes in boiling water. Strain the mushroom soaking liquid into the soup for extra flavour.

1. Heat the oil in a pan and fry the tofu on all sides until crisp and golden brown. Remove from the heat and drain on kitchen paper.

2. Put the stock in a large pan and bring to the boil. Add the rice wine vinegar and mirin together with the onion and simmer gently for 2 minutes.

3. Boil a separate pan of water, add the udon noodles and cook for 1 minute. Drain well and divide the noodles between 4 bowls. Add the bean sprouts, sliced chilli and spring onions.

4. Plunge the mushrooms into the simmering stock for 1 minute, remove with a slotted spoon and arrange on top of the noodles with the fried tofu. Sprinkle with the fried garlic and coriander leaves.

5. Stir the miso, if using, and shredded lime leaves into the hot stock. Ladle the stock over the contents of the bowls and serve piping hot. Serve accompanied with side dishes of soy sauce and crushed chilli flakes.

fruit & vegetable information: chillies page 57; oriental mushrooms page 50; nori seaweed (sea vegetables) page 51

udon noodle soup
with enoki mushrooms

philippine
sour fish soup

1 onion, finely chopped

2 garlic cloves, crushed

500 g (1 lb) unripe
tomatoes, quartered

1 carambola, thickly sliced

4 tablespoons lemon juice

1.2 litres (2 pints) water

3 tablespoons Thai fish sauce

750 g (1½ lb) mixed white fish

50 g (2 oz) morning glory,
roughly chopped

salt and pepper

To serve

Thai fish sauce

lime wedges

pickled green chillies

Serves 4

In the Philippine Islands, carambolas (star fruits) are used in cooking for their slightly tart flavour and are added to soups and meat dishes. This soup is known as Sinaging and is served with boiled rice.

1. Put the onion, garlic, tomatoes, carambola, lemon juice and water in a large saucepan and bring to a fast simmer. Cover the pan and simmer for 20 minutes.

2. Add the fish sauce to the pan and, with the back of a wooden spoon, break up the carambola pieces into a pulp. Add the fish and simmer gently for 8–10 minutes.

3. Add the morning glory and season to taste with salt and pepper. Serve in large bowls with extra fish sauce, lime wedges and pickled green chillies.

fruit & vegetable information: carambola page 15; morning glory page 66

prawn &
kaffir lime soup

A simple and easy-to-make Thai soup using raw tiger prawns and fragrant leaves and juice from knobbly kaffir limes. Strings of green peppercorns can be found in Thai or Asian general stores. These fleshy green peppercorns still attached to their stalks are added to Thai and Cambodian curries to add a peppery flavour, but are not eaten. If these peppercorns prove difficult to find, use peppercorns in brine available from supermarkets and tie 1 tablespoon of the drained peppercorns in a piece of muslin and add to the dish. Discard before eating.

5 red bird chillies

6 kaffir lime leaves

1 string of green peppercorns

1 lemon grass stalk, finely sliced

900 ml (1¹/₂ pints) water

2 tablespoons Thai fish sauce

2 teaspoons caster sugar

500 g (1 lb) raw tiger prawns, peeled

4 tablespoons kaffir lime juice

handful of coriander leaves

boiled rice, to serve

Serves 4

1. Put the chillies, kaffir lime leaves, peppercorns, chopped lemon grass and water in a large pan and gently bring to the boil. Boil for 10 minutes.

2. Reduce the heat and add the fish sauce and sugar. When the liquid is simmering, add the peeled prawns and simmer gently for 2–3 minutes or until the prawns have turned pink. Remove from the heat and add the lime juice and the coriander leaves. Serve the soup immediately with plain boiled rice.

vietnamese sugar cane prawns

3 garlic cloves, crushed

500 g (1 lb) raw prawns, peeled

1 teaspoon caster sugar

1 small egg white

25 g (1 oz) pork fat, diced (optional)

1 tablespoon ground roasted rice

30 cm (12 in) piece of sugar cane

50 g (2 oz) toasted sesame seeds

Dipping sauce

3 garlic cloves, crushed

3 tablespoons water

1 tablespoon Thai fish sauce

1 tablespoon lime juice

2 teaspoons brown sugar

1 tablespoon chopped roasted peanuts

2 small red chillies, finely chopped

Serves 4

Sugar cane prawns are a typical Vietnamese appetizer. They make a succulent starter or an eye-catching nibble with drinks. Raw sugar cane can be found in long lengths in Asian stores. Cut into sticks and peel off the thick skin.

1. First make the dipping sauce. Put the crushed garlic in a saucepan with the water, fish sauce, lime juice and brown sugar and gently heat to dissolve the sugar. Bring to the boil, remove from the heat and add the chopped peanuts and the chopped chilli. Leave to cool.

2. Put the garlic, raw peeled prawns, caster sugar and egg white in a food processor or blender and process until smooth. Add the pork fat, if using, and ground rice and process once more until well mixed.

3. Cut the sugar cane into 10 cm (4 in) lengths and then cut each length into four thin sticks. Cut away the outside skin of the sugar cane.

4. Take 2 tablespoons of the prawn mixture and press with wet hands into a compact oval shape. Press the mixture around a sugar cane stick like a kebab. When pressed on to the sugar cane, lay on a lightly oiled baking tray. Repeat with the remaining mixture and sugar cane sticks. Sprinkle with the toasted sesame seeds.

5. Cook in the centre of a preheated oven at 200°C (400°F), Gas Mark 6 for 20 minutes, turning once. Alternatively, slowly grill or barbecue the prawn sticks. Serve piping hot with the dipping sauce.

fruit & vegetable information: sugar cane page 76; chillies page 57

oven-roasted eddoes
with soured cream & smoked ham

16 large eddoes

2 tablespoons sea salt

1 teaspoon crushed black pepper

1 teaspoon cumin seeds

4 tablespoons olive oil

4–8 slices German smoked ham

150 ml (¹/₄ pint) soured cream or crème fraîche

handful of rocket leaves

chives, to garnish

Pesto dressing

2 garlic cloves, crushed

1 tablespoon pine kernels or pumpkin seeds

2 tablespoons finely grated Parmesan cheese

25 g (1 oz) rocket leaves

25 g (1 oz) watercress

150 ml (¹/₄ pint) olive oil

To serve

roasted tomatoes

rocket

crusty bread

Serves 4

Eddoes are rather like yams. In the oven they cook long and slow to a flavoursome, fibrous mash. Slit the cooked eddoes, top with soured cream, smoked ham and a pesto dressing. Very cosmopolitan.

1. Thinly peel the eddoes. Put the salt, black pepper and cumin seeds on a plate and mix together. Roll the damp eddoes in the salt mixture to create a light crust.

2. Place the eddoes on a baking tray, drizzle with the oil and bake in the centre of a preheated oven at 200°C (400°F), Gas Mark 6 for 50 minutes or until cooked through and tender.

3. Make the pesto dressing by processing the crushed garlic with the pine kernels or pumpkin seeds and the Parmesan in a food processor or blender. Add the rocket and watercress leaves and process until the mixture forms a rough purée. Add the olive oil and mix to a smooth dressing.

4. Remove the hot eddoes from the oven and arrange them on a plate, top with the smoked ham, a little soured cream and the pesto dressing. Serve with roasted tomatoes, rocket and crusty bread, garnished with chives.

fruit & vegetable information: eddoe page 58

bacon-wrapped
windward plantains

12 smoked streaky bacon
rashers, rinded

2 plantains

24 sage leaves

3–4 tablespoons vegetable oil

handful of watercress, to serve

Chilli tomato sauce

2 sweet onions, finely chopped

2 tablespoons olive oil

8 okra, trimmed and finely chopped

750 g (1½ lb) ripe tomatoes,
skinned, deseeded and chopped

5 tablespoons tomato purée

1 green chilli, deseeded and
finely chopped

2 tablespoons white wine vinegar

1 tablespoon brown sugar

2 tablespoons chopped parsley

Serves 3

In the Caribbean islands, plantains are a popular snack, whether deep-fried like crisps or made into the classic jerk sauce, which is smeared on chicken, pork or fish before griddling or barbecuing. These bacon-wrapped plantains make a delicious light lunch, snack or starter served with a bitter green salad.

1. Stretch each bacon rasher with the back of a knife. This will stop the bacon shrinking while cooking.

2. Peel the plantains and cut each into three equal lengths and then cut each section in half. Take two sage leaves and a rasher of bacon and wrap around each plantain piece. Secure with a cocktail stick and repeat with the remaining ingredients.

3. Brush the plantains with a little oil and slowly grill until the bacon is crisp and the plantains are cooked or bake in the oven at 200°C (400°F), Gas Mark 6 for 20–25 minutes. Keep warm.

4. Meanwhile, quickly fry the chopped onion in the oil until wilted. Add the chopped okra, tomatoes, tomato purée and the chopped chilli and stir into the hot oil. Reduce the heat and simmer gently for 5 minutes to release the tomato juices. Add the vinegar, brown sugar and parsley and simmer for a further 10 minutes. Purée the tomato sauce until smooth.

5. Serve the hot cooked plantains on a bed of watercress with a small bowl of the tomato sauce alongside.

fruit & vegetable information: chillies page 57; plaintain page 71; okra page 64

Nashi pears have a delicious juicy flavour that combines with the smoky flavour of Parma ham and tops a crisp bruschetta laced with garlic and herbs. For the best flavour, eat immediately. Serve as a light meal with salad leaves or make smaller versions and serve as an appetizer with drinks. If you prefer, use smoked chicken in place of the ham.

12 thick slices of ciabatta bread

3 garlic cloves, 1 halved and 2 crushed

8 tablespoons olive oil

2 tablespoons chopped basil

1 tablespoon chopped parsley

1 nashi pear, cored and sliced

6 slices of Parma ham, halved

2 teaspoons capers

salt and pepper

Serves 4

1. Rub the slices of bread all over with the cut surface of the halved garlic clove and place on a baking sheet.

2. Mix the crushed garlic with the olive oil, chopped basil and parsley and season to taste with salt and pepper. Dip each of the slices of bread into the herb oil and return to the baking sheet.

3. Grill the bread until beginning to turn golden brown, turning once and drizzling with extra oil, if necessary.

4. Top the warm bread with slices of nashi pear, a piece of Parma ham and capers. Grind black pepper over the top and serve.

fruit & vegetable information: nashi pear page 48

nashi pear &
parma ham bruschettas

thai
nam prik ong

1 teaspoon shrimp paste (optional)

4 shallots, finely chopped

6 red bird chillies

2 coriander roots

4 garlic cloves

2 tablespoons vegetable oil

500 g (1 lb) minced pork

2 firm tomatoes

1 teaspoon brown sugar

4 spring onions, chopped

1 tablespoon Thai fish sauce

2 tablespoons vegetable or
chicken stock

handful of chopped
coriander leaves

To serve

1 banana flower, steamed
and shredded

4 yard beans, trimmed into
10 cm (4 in) lengths

selection of raw vegetables

Serves 4–6

Fiery hot and very aromatic, this northern Thai dip is traditionally served with yard beans, steamed banana flower and assorted lettuce leaves.

1. Using a pestle and mortar or a food processor or blender, process the shrimp paste, if using, shallots, chillies, coriander roots and garlic to make a thick paste. Heat the oil in a frying pan until hot and fry the paste for 2–3 minutes to cook the shallots.

2. With the frying pan still searing hot, add the pork to the pan and stir-fry for 5–6 minutes or until the pork is cooked through. Add the tomatoes, sugar, spring onions, fish sauce and stock and simmer for a further 5 minutes.

3. Leave the dip to cool a little, then mix in the coriander. Serve surrounded by shredded banana flower, yard beans and a selection of raw vegetables.

fruit & vegetable information: chillies page 57; banana flower page 72; yard bean page 61

laotian
som tam

Green papaya has a sharp flavour and strong texture and is commonly eaten as a vegetable in South-east Asia as much as its riper cousin is eaten as a fresh fruit. Here it is combined in a salad with yard beans. You will need a large pestle and mortar for this recipe but, failing that, pound the papaya with the end of a rolling pin in a heavy-based bowl. The idea is to amalgamate the flavours into the tough green papaya and to make the papaya easier to digest.

375 g (12 oz) green papaya

2 garlic cloves

3 red bird chillies

4 cherry tomatoes

4 yard beans, cut into 5 cm (2 in) lengths

2 tablespoons Thai fish sauce

2 teaspoons caster sugar

2 tablespoons lime juice

1 tablespoon dried shrimps

3 tablespoons chopped roasted peanuts

handful of coriander

Serves 4

1. Peel the papaya and roughly grate the flesh or cut into fine shreds.

2. Place the garlic, chillies and cherry tomatoes in a large mortar and pound to a rough purée with a pestle.

3. Add the grated papaya, yard beans, fish sauce, sugar, lime juice and dried shrimps and pound together until roughly mixed.

4. Add the chopped peanuts and coriander and serve.

1 small daikon

3 carrots, peeled

1 large, firm red pepper

1 tablespoon sesame seeds, toasted

1 teaspoon sesame oil

1 tablespoon mirin

1 tablespoon rice wine vinegar

4 spring onions, thinly shredded

coriander leaves, to garnish

Serves 4

A succulent, fresh Japanese-inspired coleslaw of finely shredded vegetables. Each vegetable adds its own sweet and flavoursome characteristics. The best way to prepare them is to have a mandolin in which to shred the vegetables. Failing that, grate along the length of each of the vegetables to obtain the longest strands possible. Add the dressing just before serving, while still warm.

1. Grate or shred the daikon, carrots and red pepper. If the red pepper proves difficult to shred, thinly slice into julienne strips. Place all the vegetables and the sesame seeds in a bowl and mix everything together with your hands.

2. Put the sesame oil, mirin and vinegar in a small pan and heat gently for 2–3 minutes to combine the flavours. Remove the pan from the heat and allow to cool a little.

3. Arrange the salad in a mound in the centre of each of 4 plates and pour the dressing over and around the salad. Top each salad with finely shredded spring onions. Serve garnished with coriander leaves.

fruit & vegetable information: daikon page 75

daikon, carrot & red pepper

with toasted sesame dressing

feta, rocket &
kiwiano salad

The combination of salty feta cheese, fragrant cucumber-flavoured kiwiano and sweet cherry tomatoes matches the complexity of rocket leaves and assertive mint sprigs. A salad bouncing with flavour, texture and colour. Serve with side dishes of olives, sun-dried tomatoes and capers.

250 g (8 oz) feta cheese, drained

2 teaspoons crushed mixed peppercorns

6 tablespoons extra virgin olive oil

12 cherry or baby plum tomatoes, halved

1/2 cucumber, diced

handful of mint leaves

handful of wild rocket leaves

1 kiwiano

1 tablespoon balsamic vinegar

sea salt and pepper

Serves 4

1. Cut the feta into thick slices or dice. Sprinkle the crushed peppercorns over the cheese and drizzle with 2 tablespoons of the oil.

2. Gently mix the feta, cherry tomatoes and diced cucumber together. Arrange the mint and rocket leaves on a plate and top with the feta and tomatoes.

3. Cut the kiwiano in half, scoop out the seeds and sprinkle over the salad.

4. Mix the remaining olive oil with the balsamic vinegar. Season to taste with salt and pepper and drizzle over the salad.

fruit & vegetable information: kiwiano page 24

smoked chicken &
mustard leaf salad with rambutans

Rambutans look great just peeled and still sitting in their spiky defensive cloaks. These sweet pods combine well with smoked chicken and sharp-tasting leaves to make an attention-seeking salad with plenty of impact.

50 g (2 oz) mustard leaves or watercress

25 g (1 oz) mizuna or rocket

handful of purslane (optional)

125 g (4 oz) smoked chicken, thinly sliced

8 rambutans

chives, to garnish

Dressing

2 tablespoons virgin olive oil

1/2 teaspoon Dijon mustard

1 teaspoon caster sugar

1/2 teaspoon paprika

1 tablespoon chopped dill

sea salt and pepper

Serves 4

1. Arrange the mustard leaves, mizuna and purslane, if using, in the centre of a plate. Place the slices of smoked chicken over the top of the leaves.

2. Peel back the skin of the rambutans and arrange around the salad.

3. Make the dressing by mixing the olive oil, mustard, caster sugar and paprika together. Stir in the dill and season to taste with salt and pepper.

4. Drizzle the dressing over and around the salad and serve immediately, garnished with chives.

fruit & vegetable information: rambutan page 39

longans with
ginger & lime syrup

Half sweet, half savoury, this salad can be served as a starter, main course or dessert. The lime syrup is not excessively sweet and, together with the impact of the fresh ginger, is packed with a punch that lifts the longans into an aromatic state that can take on air-cured hams, salad leaves or ice cream. You decide.

40 g (1¹/₂ oz) caster sugar

150 ml (¹/₄ pint) cold water

4 kaffir lime leaves

finely grated rind and juice of 3 limes

7 cm (3 in) piece of fresh root ginger, finely grated or cut into julienne strips

30 fresh or 400 g (13 oz) can longans

4 bruised lemon grass stalks

Serves 4

1. Put the caster sugar in a pan with the water and gently heat to dissolve the sugar. Increase the heat, stop stirring and bring to the boil. Boil for 5 minutes until a light syrup is formed. Add the lime leaves and remove from the heat.

2. Add the lime juice, finely grated rind and root ginger to the syrup and leave to stand until the syrup is cold.

3. Peel the longans, remove the central stone and add to the syrup with the lemon grass. Serve in small glasses or bowls.

fruit & vegetable information: longan page 29

toasted peanut, mint,
pomelo & king prawn salad

Pomelos have a mild grapefruit flavour which combines well with the prawns, toasted peanut and fish sauce flavours. The salad can be served in the hollowed-out pomelo shells; this makes an attractive table piece for a Thai-inspired supper.

1 large pomelo

125 g (4 oz) peanuts, toasted and roughly chopped

175 g (6 oz) raw tiger prawns, peeled

2 tablespoons grapefruit juice

1/2 tablespoon Thai fish sauce

4 spring onions, finely shredded

6 mint leaves, finely shredded

1 large red chilli, finely sliced

pinch of crushed chilli or black pepper

pinch of grated nutmeg

4–5 frisée or lollo rosso leaves

Serves 4

1. Cut the pomelo in half and scoop out the segments and juice. Discard the pith and thick skin surrounding each segment and break the flesh into small pieces. Stir the toasted peanuts into the pomelo flesh and set aside to allow the flavours to blend.

2. Bring a pan of water to the boil and simmer the prawns for 1–2 minutes, or until the prawns turn pink and are cooked through.

3. Remove the prawns with a slotted spoon and drain well. Add the prawns to the pomelo flesh with the grapefruit juice, fish sauce, shredded spring onions and mint.

4. Sprinkle the finely sliced chilli, crushed chilli or pepper and nutmeg over the salad and toss together. Line the inside of a bowl with the lettuce leaves and spoon in the salad. Serve immediately.

fruit & vegetable information: pomelo page 20; chillies page 57

A bright summer salad with hard, crumbly cheese, richly flavoured air-dried ham and the unusual sweet intensity of prickly pears. Add salad leaves of your choice, but the assertive flavours of watercress and chervil are best to match the other complex flavours in the salad. Serve with chilled red wine and crusty bread.

4 prickly pears

125 g (4 oz) haloumi cheese, thickly sliced

4 slices of Italian air-dried ham

50 g (2 oz) watercress or mizuna leaves

1 large red chilli, deseeded and finely chopped

2 tablespoons lime juice

2 tablespoons black olives

handful of chervil sprigs

sea salt and pepper

Dressing

2 tablespoons extra virgin olive oil

1 tablespoon orange juice

1 tablespoon sherry vinegar

pinch of crushed chilli

Serves 4

1. Wearing plastic gloves, cut each of the prickly pears in half and then into quarters. Remove the skins if preferred, taking care with the small hairy spikes.

2. Put some haloumi cheese in the centre of each plate and arrange the Italian ham and prickly pear on top of the cheese along with the watercress or mizuna. Sprinkle with the chilli, salt and pepper and the lime juice. Scatter olives around the plate and add the chervil.

3. Make the dressing by mixing the olive oil, orange juice, sherry vinegar and crushed chilli together. Just before serving, drizzle a little of the dressing over the salad and serve immediately.

fruit & vegetable information: prickly pear page 40; chillies page 57

prickly pear salad with
cured ham & haloumi cheese

baked congo potatoes
with pancetta & coriander butter

These purple potatoes make the most eye-catching mash ever seen. Also try making them into potato cakes with fish or sausages and watch everyone's faces as you hand them a plate. They have a waxy, dense texture and a somewhat sweet flavour. Quite delicious. Here they are simply baked and served with a coriander butter and pancetta and are ideal as a side dish to accompany omelettes, quiches or cooked meats.

500 g (1 lb) Congo potatoes

75 g (3 oz) pancetta or smoked streaky bacon, cut into strips

sea salt and pepper

coriander leaves, to garnish

Coriander butter

2 tablespoons lemon juice

1 tablespoon chopped coriander

50 g (2 oz) softened salted butter

1/2 teaspoon crushed black pepper

pinch of chilli flakes

Serves 4

1. Wash the potatoes, cut any large ones in half and spread across an ovenproof dish and sprinkle with sea salt. Bake in a preheated oven at 190°C (375°F), Gas Mark 5 for 50 minutes or until the potatoes are tender and cooked through.

2. Make the butter by beating the lemon juice and chopped coriander into the softened butter together with the black pepper and chilli flakes. Shape the butter into a narrow log, roll in greaseproof paper and chill until required.

3. Heat a heavy-based frying pan until hot and add the pancetta or bacon and fry until crisp.

4. Remove the potatoes from the oven, sprinkle the pancetta over the top and season to taste with pepper. Cut the coriander butter into slices, place on top of the potatoes and serve garnished with coriander leaves.

fruit & vegetable information: South American blue potatoes (Congo potatoes) page 78

750 g (1½ lb) dudhi

4 tablespoons vegetable oil

1 teaspoon ground cumin

1 teaspoon garam masala

½ teaspoon turmeric

½ teaspoon hot paprika

2 large carrots, peeled and finely chopped

50 g (2 oz) peas, thawed if frozen

6–8 fresh curry leaves

25 g (1 oz) brown sugar

300 ml (½ pint) vegetable stock or water

handful of coriander leaves

salt and pepper

mint sprig, to garnish

brown basmati rice, to serve

Raita

150 ml (¼ pint) thick set yogurt

1 tablespoon chopped mint

10 cm (4 in) piece of cucumber, finely diced or grated

2 tomatoes, deseeded and finely chopped

Serves 6

west indian
spiced dudhi

Dudhi is a long, tapered gourd that is delicious when cooked with a variety of spices and herbs. This is a simple vegetable curry, ideal to serve with rice or as a side dish with a meat curry or tandoori chicken.

1. Wash and thinly peel the dudhi. Cut in half and scoop out the seeds, then cut the flesh into cubes or batons.

2. Heat the oil in a large saucepan and add the cumin, garam masala, turmeric and paprika. Lightly fry the spices and then add the prepared dudhi, carrots and peas. Cook over a high heat for 2–3 minutes to lightly brown the vegetables.

3. Add the curry leaves, brown sugar and vegetable stock and simmer gently for 15 minutes.

4. Meanwhile make the raita by mixing the yogurt with the mint, cucumber and chopped tomato and season to taste with salt and pepper. Chill until required and mix well before serving.

5. When the vegetables are cooked but still retain their texture, season to taste with salt and pepper and stir in the coriander leaves. Serve with brown basmati rice and top with the raita and a sprig of mint.

fruit & vegetable information: dudhi page 67

sautéed salsify in black nut
butter with flat leaf parsley

Salsify makes an ideal accompaniment to roast meat or a winter stew. Cook the butter long and slow until it turns a beautiful nut-brown colour. Do not allow it to go too far, or the butter will taste burnt. Just as it begins to reach the right colour, remove from the heat and allow to continue cooking in the residual heat of the pan.

3 shallots, finely chopped

2 tablespoons vegetable oil

500 g (1 lb) salsify

2 tablespoons lemon juice

50 g (2 oz) salted butter

2 tablespoons chopped flat leaf parsley

salt and pepper

Serves 4

1. Put the shallots in a small pan with the oil and fry gently until wilted.

2. Scrub the salsify to remove any dirt and thinly peel. Cut the salsify into 7 cm (3 in) lengths or into thick julienne or batons and drop immediately into water with lemon juice or vinegar added – this stops them browning.

3. Bring a pan of water to the boil and add the salsify. Boil for 5 minutes or until tender when tested with the tip of a sharp knife. Drain well.

4. Add the drained salsify to the fried shallots and heat through in the pan. Squeeze the lemon juice over the salsify and season to taste with salt and pepper. Cover with a lid and leave to warm through.

5. Melt the butter in a small pan and then gently heat until the butter turns a nut-brown colour. Remove immediately from the heat and pour over the salsify. Sprinkle with the chopped parsley and serve.

500 g (1 lb) karela

2 teaspoons salt

3 large sweet onions

1 large aubergine, diced

4 tablespoons vegetable oil

1 teaspoon turmeric

1 teaspoon ground coriander

1 teaspoon garam masala

1/2 teaspoon mild paprika

3 garlic cloves, crushed

3 tablespoons soft brown sugar

1 tablespoon tamarind paste

300 ml (1/2 pint) vegetable
stock or water

1 tablespoon grated fresh coconut
or 1/2 tablespoon desiccated coconut

150 ml (1/4 pint) thick Greek yogurt
or crème fraîche

salt and pepper

rice, to serve

handful of coriander, to garnish

Serves 4

karela sautéed
with tamarind

Karela are bright green, tapered vegetables covered in ridges. They contain a sticky sap, similar to okra, and bitter juices. It is well worth soaking the prepared slices in salt water to remove some of this bitterness. Cook in a creamy turmeric sauce and serve alongside Middle Eastern fish or chicken dishes, with oven-baked breads and chutneys.

1. Trim the karela, cut in half, scoop out the seeds and the white pulp and then thinly slice. Put the slices in a bowl of water with the salt. Leave for 1 hour, then drain.

2. Gently fry the onions and diced aubergine in the oil for about 20 minutes, stirring frequently. When the onions are caramelized and the aubergines are golden brown, add the turmeric, coriander, garam masala and paprika and gently fry for a further 2 minutes.

3. Add the drained karela to the spices with the garlic, brown sugar, tamarind paste and stock or water. Cover and simmer gently for 8 minutes.

4. Season to taste with salt and pepper, add the coconut and simmer gently for a further 5 minutes. Remove from the heat and stir in the yogurt or crème fraîche. Serve with plain boiled or pilau rice topped with coriander leaves.

fruit & vegetable information: coconut page 23; karela page 69; aubergine page 79

Pak bung fadang, *as it is known in Thailand, is an everyday Thai vegetable dish. In the street markets of Bangkok and village market places around the country, this dish is cooked at super speed with flames often dancing around the vast woks in which it is tossed. At home, just get the wok or frying pan as smoking hot as possible and have all the ingredients ready to go into the pan. Serve immediately.*

2 tablespoons vegetable oil

1 garlic clove, sliced

1 red bird chilli

300 g (10 oz) morning glory, roughly chopped

125 g (4 oz) peeled raw prawns

3 tablespoons light soy sauce

2 teaspoons caster sugar

1 tablespoon rice wine

1 tablespoon Thai fish sauce

6 tablespoons water

Chinese chive flowers, to garnish

Serves 4

1. Heat the oil in a wok or large frying pan and add the sliced garlic clove and chilli. Stir-fry for 30 seconds.

2. Add the morning glory and prawns and stir-fry in the oil for 1–2 minutes until the morning glory begins to wilt and the prawns are pink and cooked through.

3. Mix the soy sauce, sugar, rice wine, fish sauce and water together and add to the pan. Quickly stir-fry together for another minute and serve while the morning glory still has texture. Top with Chinese chive flowers.

fruit & vegetable information: chillies page 57; morning glory page 66; Chinese chive page 53

stir-fried morning glory
with garlic & chilli

okra, yogurt & turmeric with corncakes

2 large onions, chopped

3 tablespoons vegetable oil

1 teaspoon each black onion seeds, cumin seeds, turmeric

500 g (1 lb) okra, trimmed

250 g (8 oz) tomatoes, chopped

2 tablespoons tomato purée

150 ml (¼ pint) vegetable stock or water

2 tablespoons chopped coriander, plus extra to garnish

4 tablespoons thick Greek yogurt

salt and pepper

Corncakes

50 g (2 oz) plain flour

125 g (4 oz) cornmeal

1 small egg, beaten

150 ml (¼ pint) milk or water

1 green chilli, deseeded and finely chopped

125 g (4 oz) sweetcorn kernels

6–12 tablespoons vegetable oil, for shallow-frying

Serves 4–6

Okra is very popular in the deep south of the USA in fried dishes and prawn gumbos. Here it is cooked in Asian spices and finished at the last moment with a cooling addition of thick set, creamy yogurt. Serve on southern-style sweetcorn fritters – just like an all-American grandma would make.

1. Fry the onion in the oil until beginning to wilt. Add the onion seeds, cumin seeds and turmeric. Fry gently until the onion seeds begin to pop.

2. Cut the okra in half lengthways, add to the hot pan and toss in the spices. Add the tomatoes, tomato purée and the stock or water and simmer gently for 8–10 minutes.

3. Make the batter for the corncakes by processing the plain flour, cornmeal, beaten egg and milk in a food processor or blender until smooth. Alternatively, combine the ingredients with a whisk. Stir in the chopped chilli, salt and pepper and the sweetcorn kernels. Set aside to stand for 20 minutes.

4. Heat the oil for shallow-frying until a cube of bread dropped in the oil turns golden brown in 3 minutes. Carefully spoon large tablespoons of the sweetcorn batter into the hot oil and fry for 6 minutes, turning occasionally.

5. Remove from the oil with a slotted spoon and drain on kitchen paper. Stir the chopped coriander into the okra and serve the okra spooned on top of the corncakes. Add a spoonful of yogurt, garnish with coriander leaves and serve immediately.

fruit & vegetable information: okra page 64; chillies page 57

braised pak choi
with black bean & chilli sauce

Pak choi or any other leafy Chinese vegetable can be used in this dish. It is a simple grouping of all the ingredients most loved in Chinese cooking, packed with vitamins and minerals. Keep the vegetable as crisp as possible by briefly cooking in boiling water and then stir-frying in the hot oil with garlic cloves and fried tofu.

750 g (1¹/₂ lb) pak choi, trimmed

1 head of garlic

150 ml (¹/₄ pint) water

1. Cut any large pak choi in half or quarters and rinse well. Break the head of garlic into cloves and place in a saucepan with the water. Bring to the boil. Stand the pak choi upright in the pan of boiling water and leave to cook for 5 minutes.

3 tablespoons groundnut or vegetable oil

2. Remove the pak choi from the pan and drain. Remove the garlic from the boiling water and slip the cloves out of the skins. Reserve the boiling water.

125 g (4 oz) tofu, drained and cut into chunks

1 large red chilli, deseeded and finely chopped

3. Heat the oil in a wok, add the tofu and cook on all sides. Remove and reserve. Add the pak choi to the hot oil and toss in the oil for 2 minutes. Add the chopped chilli and the garlic cloves.

2 tablespoons black bean sauce

1 tablespoon oyster sauce

2 tablespoons light soy sauce

boiled rice, to serve

4. Working quickly, mix the black bean, oyster and soy sauces together with 6–8 tablespoons of the reserved vegetable water. Pour this mixture over the pak choi and toss together. Add the fried tofu and toss again carefully. Serve immediately with plain boiled rice.

Serves 4

fruit & vegetable information: pak choi page 56; chillies page 57

250 g (8 oz) water chestnuts, thinly peeled

1 tablespoon caster sugar

1/2 teaspoon black pepper

2 tablespoons vegetable oil

1 sweet white onion, thickly sliced

250 g (8 oz) fresh mussels

125 g (4 oz) raw tiger prawns, peeled

4 spring onions, trimmed and diagonally sliced

1/2 teaspoon crushed chilli flakes

125 g (4 oz) sugar snap peas, trimmed and diagonally halved

125 g (4 oz) bean sprouts

3 tablespoons soy sauce

2 tablespoons yellow bean sauce

2 tablespoons Shaosing wine or sherry

chervil sprigs, to garnish

To serve

boiled rice

bean sprouts

dried crushed chilli flakes

lime wedges

Serves 4

Water chestnuts add a much appreciated crisp crunch to stir-fries. Their delicate nutty flavour is perfect with seafood and vegetables. Don't overcook this dish as it loses its edge. Make it at the last moment and serve it piping hot with side plates of fresh bean sprouts, dried crushed chilli flakes and lime wedges.

1. Thickly slice the water chestnuts, sprinkle with the sugar and pepper and set aside.

2. Heat the oil in a large frying pan or wok, add the onion and mussels and stir-fry quickly for 1 minute. Put a lid on the pan and cook for 3–4 minutes or until the mussels have opened. Discard any mussels that remain closed.

3. Add the water chestnuts, prawns, spring onions, chilli flakes, sugar snaps and bean sprouts to the pan and stir fry for 1–2 minutes or until the prawns have turned pink and are cooked through.

4. Mix together the soy sauce, yellow bean sauce and wine or sherry and pour over the ingredients in the wok. Stir-fry for a further 1–2 minutes until hot. Serve with plain boiled rice, bean sprouts, chilli flakes, lime wedges and garnish with chervil sprigs.

fruit & vegetable information: water chestnut page 62

water chestnut,
sugar snap & seafood stir-fry

red snapper roasted
with sweet elephant garlic

*These large heads of garlic are sweet and creamy and
make a delicious accompaniment to fish, chicken or lamb.
Roast the heads of garlic whole or in individual cloves and
cook alongside Mediterranean vegetables. If red snapper is
hard to find, substitute with monkfish or even salmon.*

1 large head of elephant garlic

1 head of fennel, cut into thick slices

8 baby aubergines, halved

**1 red pepper, deseeded and
roughly chopped**

**1 orange pepper, deseeded and
roughly chopped**

150 ml (¼ pint) olive oil

15 g (½ oz) basil leaves

**1 red chilli, deseeded and
finely chopped**

**750 g (1½ lb) red snapper
fillets, scaled**

finely grated rind of 1 lemon or lime

**2 tablespoons chopped
flat leaf parsley**

salt and pepper

chives, to garnish

Serves 4

1. Break the garlic into single cloves and lay in a
baking tin. Add the sliced fennel, aubergines and red
and orange peppers.

2. Drizzle about 3 tablespoons of the olive oil over the
vegetables, season with salt and pepper and roast in
the centre of a preheated oven at 200°C (400°F), Gas
Mark 6 for 30 minutes, turning once.

3. Put the remaining oil in a small pan with the
basil leaves and chopped chilli and heat gently for
5 minutes. Remove from the heat and allow to cool.
When cold, remove the basil leaves and discard.

4. Rub the red snapper fillets with a little oil and
season with salt, pepper and the grated lemon or
lime rind. Place the fish on top of the roasting
vegetables and cook in the centre of the oven for a
further 12–15 minutes.

5. Serve the fish on a bed of the roasted garlic and
vegetables. Drizzle a little basil and chilli oil around
and over the fish, garnish with chives and serve.

These are very easy to make. The sweetness from the potatoes marries well with the crabmeat; the mixture shapes into perfect round cakes that are pan-fried and served with a garlicky mayonnaise. Great as a main course, or roll the mixture into small balls and serve as an appetizer with drinks. Prepare well in advance and chill in the refrigerator before frying to ensure they remain firm and hold their shape. Keep warm in the oven while cooking the remainder or waiting for guests to arrive.

500 g (1 lb) sweet potatoes

250 g (8 oz) King Edward potatoes

1 small egg, beaten

250 g (8 oz) crabmeat

¹/₂ teaspoon pimento picante or paprika

3 tablespoons plain flour

oil, for shallow-frying

salt and pepper

salad leaves, to serve

Garlic mayonnaise

2 garlic cloves, crushed

1 small red chilli, deseeded and chopped

1 medium egg yolk

1 tablespoon white wine vinegar

150 ml (¹/₄ pint) olive oil

Serves 4

1. Peel the potatoes and cook in boiling water for about 10 minutes or until soft when pierced with the tip of a knife. Drain well, return to the pan and roughly mash.

2. Add the beaten egg, season with salt and pepper and mix well. Add the crabmeat and mix into the potato mash with the pimento or paprika and flour.

3. With floured hands, shape 2 tablespoons of the mixture into a potato cake. Repeat until all the mixture has been used, then chill in the refrigerator for 1–2 hours.

4. Heat the oil in a large frying pan and fry 4 potato cakes at a time for 3–4 minutes, turning occasionally, until the potato cakes are golden brown on all sides and heated through. Remove from the oil and drain well. Keep warm while cooking the remainder.

5. To make the garlic mayonnaise, put the crushed garlic and chilli in a food processor or blender with the egg yolk and vinegar and process well. With the motor still running slowly add the olive oil in a thin stream. If this is added slowly enough, the egg mixture will gradually thicken into a mayonnaise.

6. Serve the warm potato cakes with a large spoonful of the mayonnaise and a mixture of crisp salad leaves.

fruit & vegetable information: sweet potato page 65; chillies page 57

crab & sweet potato
fish cakes

pomfret with coconut
& tamarind sambal

1 small lemon grass stalk

2 garlic cloves, crushed

6 tablespoons grated fresh coconut
or 50 g (2 oz) desiccated coconut

2 green chillies, deseeded and
finely chopped

4 small pomfret, descaled and
gutted and flesh slashed

4 tablespoons vegetable oil

handful of coriander leaves

lemon wedges

boiled rice

Coconut & tamarind sambal

1 onion, finely chopped

1 garlic clove, crushed

1 tablespoon vegetable oil

2 tablespoons grated fresh coconut

1 red chilli, deseeded and
finely chopped

150 ml (¼ pint) boiling water

2 tablespoons dried tamarind pulp

2 teaspoons caster sugar

1 tablespoon white wine vinegar

1 tablespoon chopped coriander

Serves 4

These comical-looking fish can be found in Asian stores either fresh or frozen. If hard to find, substitute with plaice or other delicate white fish. The grated coconut makes an interesting crisp coating which perfumes the fish as it marinates. The sambal is sweet and sour and adds another dimension to the dish. If time is tight, serve the fish with mango chutney instead.

1. Finely chop the lemon grass stalk and mix with the crushed garlic, grated coconut and green chillies until combined. Smear this dry mixture over each pomfret, cover and chill in the refrigerator for 2 hours or overnight to marinate.

2. Make the coconut and tamarind sambal by gently frying the onion and garlic in the oil until wilted. Add the grated coconut with the chilli, coat in the oil and cook for 2–3 minutes. Pour the boiling water over the tamarind pulp and leave to stand for 10 minutes to dissolve.

3. Strain the juice from the tamarind pulp, mashing as much of the pulp through the sieve as possible. Add this juice to the pan with the sugar and simmer gently for 5 minutes. Add the vinegar, remove from the heat and leave to cool. When cold stir in the chopped coriander.

4. Heat the oil in a large frying pan and gently fry the pomfret, 2 at a time in the hot oil, turning once. After 6–8 minutes, when the pomfret are golden brown and cooked, remove from the oil and drain on kitchen paper. Alternatively grill the pomfret for 10 minutes until golden brown and cooked. Keep warm in a hot oven while cooking the remaining fish. Serve the fish piping hot with the coconut and tamarind sambal, coriander, lemon wedges and plain boiled rice.

braised chinese chives
with seafood

When roughly chopped and added to soups or prawn and fish dishes, Chinese chives add a delicious strong onion flavour. Here they are stir-fried with seafood to make a light and delicate dish to serve with plain rice. The first time I tasted this was in Thailand where these chives grow in abundance.

175 g (6 oz) Chinese chives

175 g (6 oz) raw tiger prawns

3 squid tubes

3 garlic cloves

1 red chilli, deseeded

1 green chilli, deseeded

2 tablespoons vegetable oil

2 tablespoons light soy sauce

1 tablespoon oyster sauce

handful of coriander

white or brown rice, to serve

Serves 4

1. Rinse the chives and roughly chop into 2.5 cm (1 in) lengths.

2. Peel the prawns, leaving on the tips of the tails. Cut the squid tubes in half and, using a sharp knife, make a series of criss-cross cuts into the outside of the squid flesh, taking care not to cut right through.

3. Using the back of a heavy knife, crush the garlic cloves and then finely chop them along with the red and green chillies.

4. Heat the oil in a large cast-iron pan or wok. Add the squid and cook on all sides until slightly charred and cooked through.

5. Add the garlic, chillies and the prawns to the pan and stir-fry for 1 minute. Add the chopped chives and stir-fry quickly for 2 minutes or until the prawns are pink and cooked through. Add the soy sauce and oyster sauce and stir-fry for 1 further minute. Add the coriander leaves and serve immediately with plain white or brown rice.

fruit & vegetable information: Chinese chive page 53; chillies page 57

west indian ackee
& pigeon pea curry

2 red onions, sliced

2 tablespoons vegetable oil

250 g (8 oz) tomatoes, chopped

1 thyme sprig

1/2 teaspoon chilli powder

1/2 teaspoon grated nutmeg

125 g (4 oz) dried pigeon or gungo
peas, soaked overnight

600 ml (1 pint) vegetable stock
or water

500 g (1 lb) can ackee, drained

6 anchovy fillets, chopped

2 tablespoons chopped parsley

salt and pepper

To serve

boiled rice

thick papaya or pineapple slices

Serves 4

Ackee is most commonly found in cans – it resembles large pieces of scrambled egg and is added to Jamaican vegetable curries along with dried beans and lentils. Pigeon or gungo peas can also be found in cans or dried. If using canned peas, add them to the curry towards the end of cooking time, together with the ackee, and don't overcook to a mush. Try and keep the ackee and peas whole if possible.

1. Put the onions and vegetable oil in a large saucepan and cook until the onion has wilted. Add the chopped tomatoes together with the thyme, chilli powder, grated nutmeg and soaked pigeon peas. Cover the pan and simmer for 5 minutes.

2. Add the stock or water to the pan and bring to the boil. Continue to boil for 10 minutes, reduce the heat and simmer for a further 20 minutes or until the pigeon peas are cooked through. Add extra stock or water, if necessary.

3. Add the ackee, anchovies and chopped parsley to the tomato sauce and heat gently for 8 minutes. Season to taste with salt and pepper and serve with boiled rice and papaya or pineapple slices.

fruit & vegetable information: ackee page 55; papaya page 17; queen pineapple 13

jackfruit & coconut
curry with chicken

In South-east Asia, jackfruit trees grow in many gardens and are harvested as the giant pods ripen. This jackfruit curry (Nasi campur) is an everyday staple in Sumatra, Indonesia. The jackfruit is gently cooked in a broth of mildly spiced coconut. This same curry base can be used with shredded banana flower or hard-boiled eggs.

2 garlic cloves, crushed

2 lemon grass stalks, crushed

7 cm (3 in) piece of galangal or fresh root ginger, peeled and finely chopped

2 green chillies, deseeded and finely chopped

1 teaspoon coriander seeds

3 tablespoons vegetable oil

300 ml (½ pint) coconut milk

150 ml (¼ pint) water

4 kaffir lime leaves

175 g (6 oz) skinless chicken breast, thinly sliced

400 g (13 oz) jackfruit flesh, chopped or 625g (1¼ lb) can jackfruit, drained

2 strings of green peppercorns

1 red chilli, deseeded and finely chopped

handful of coriander

Serves 4

1. Put the garlic, lemon grass, galangal or ginger, green chillies and coriander seeds in a food processor or blender and process to a smooth paste.

2. Heat the oil in a large saucepan, add the curry paste and cook while stirring for 2–3 minutes. Reduce the heat and add the coconut milk, water and 3 shredded lime leaves. Simmer gently for 10 minutes.

3. Add the sliced chicken, jackfruit and peppercorns and simmer gently for 6–8 minutes or until the chicken has cooked through. Stir in the chopped red chilli and coriander and serve garnished with the remaining lime leaf.

125 g (4 oz) flaked almonds

50 g (2 oz) peanuts

1/2 tablespoon coriander seeds

1 teaspoon ground cloves

3 tablespoons sesame seeds

1/2 cinnamon stick

1 teaspoon fennel or aniseed

4 large dried chillies

1 green jalapeño chilli, chopped

400 g (13 oz) can chopped tomatoes

75 g (3 oz) raisins

6 tablespoons vegetable oil

2 onions, finely chopped

3 garlic cloves, crushed

625 g (1¼ lb) turkey fillets, finely sliced or cubed

300 ml (1/2 pint) vegetable stock or water

50 g (2 oz) bitter plain chocolate, roughly chopped

To garnish

1 red and 1 green chilli, finely chopped

handful of coriander

Serves 6

Chilli-hot dishes are all the rage in South America and this is one of their most interesting ones. A slow-cooked dish of turkey with hot chillies and bitter plain chocolate, thickened with ground almonds. It is a fascinating combination that works well.

1. Spread the almonds, peanuts, coriander seeds, cloves, sesame seeds, cinnamon, fennel or aniseed and dried chillies over a baking sheet and roast in a preheated oven at 200°C (400°F), Gas Mark 6 for 10 minutes, stirring once or twice.

2. Remove from the oven and put the nuts and spices in a food processor or blender and process until well combined. Add the chopped green chilli and process once more until well mixed.

3. Spoon the spice mixture into a bowl and mix in the tomatoes and raisins.

4. Heat the oil in a large saucepan and fry the onion and garlic with the turkey on all sides until brown. Remove the turkey and set aside.

5. Add the spice mixture to the oil remaining in the saucepan and fry, stirring frequently, for 5–6 minutes or until the spice paste has heated through and begun to brown. Add the stock and chocolate and simmer gently until the chocolate has melted.

6. Reduce the heat, return the turkey to the pan and mix well. Cover the pan and simmer gently for 30 minutes, adding extra water if the sauce begins to dry out. Garnish with chopped red and green chillies and coriander.

fruit & vegetable information: chillies page 57

turkey
chilli poblano

thai
jungle curry.

600 ml (1 pint) water

1 tablespoon ready-made
Thai red curry paste

2 teaspoons caster sugar

1 teaspoon salt

6 small round green aubergines

2 baby purple aubergines, halved

10–12 pea aubergines

50 g (2 oz) green beans

8 kaffir lime leaves

5 cm (2 in) piece of galangal

6 baby sweetcorn, halved

3 strings of green peppercorns

2 large green chillies

20 fresh lychees or 400 g (13 oz)
can lychees

12 holy basil leaves

boiled white rice, to serve

Serves 4

Out in the northern reaches of Thailand, Burma and Laos, meat is at a premium and the average curry dish contains vegetables and seeds collected from the jungles that surround the villages. They are cooked together in a spicy aromatic broth flavoured with red curry paste. This paste is now easy to find ready-made in Asian shops and most large supermarkets.

1. Put the water in a saucepan and bring to the boil. Stir the red curry paste into the water with sugar and salt and return to the boil.

2. Reduce the heat and add the aubergines, green beans, lime leaves, galangal, sweetcorn, peppercorns and green chillies and simmer gently for 5 minutes.

3. Add the lychees and basil leaves to the saucepan and simmer for a further 2 minutes. Remove the galangal and serve the curry while still hot with plenty of plain white rice.

hot indian tindori
& green mango curry

125 g (4 oz) dried green lentils, rinsed

These little bitter pods are used in northern Indian cooking with lentils and hot spices. They are added to a simple tomato-based curry and simmered until just cooked. Just before serving, shredded green mango and red onion are added to the dish with coriander leaves.

1 teaspoon turmeric

2 teaspoons garam masala

1 teaspoon each, cumin seeds and black onion seeds

1. Add the rinsed lentils to a saucepan of boiling water, return to the boil and cook for 20 minutes. Drain.

3 tablespoons vegetable oil

1 red chilli, finely chopped

2. Put the turmeric, garam masala, cumin seeds and black onion seeds in a pan with the oil and fry for 1–2 minutes or until the spices are sizzling and the mustard seeds begin to pop.

1 green chilli, finely chopped

3 large tomatoes, chopped

3. Add the chopped chillies and the tomatoes together with the drained lentils and tindori. Cover the pan and simmer gently for 10 minutes, stirring occasionally.

250 g (8 oz) tindori, rinsed and trimmed

2 tablespoons soft brown sugar

4. Mix the brown sugar and tamarind paste with the boiling water and add to the pan. Stir well and simmer for a further 5 minutes. Season to taste with salt and pepper.

1 tablespoon tamarind paste

150 ml (¼ pint) boiling water

5. Shred the mango finely and mix with the red onion and coriander leaves. Serve the tindori curry with chapati, topped with the green mango and red onion mixture and garnish with flat leaf parsley sprigs.

1 small green mango

1 small red onion, finely chopped

handful of coriander leaves, chopped

salt and pepper

chapati, to serve

flat leaf parsley sprigs, to garnish

Serves 4

fruit & vegetable information: green mango page 36; chillies page 57; tindori page 81

indian drumstick
masala curry

1 teaspoon mustard seeds

1 teaspoon garam masala

4 small pieces of cassia bark

1/2 teaspoon ground coriander

1/2 teaspoon ground cumin

1/2 teaspoon hot paprika

1/2 teaspoon turmeric

2 onions, chopped

6 tablespoons vegetable oil

2 garlic cloves, crushed

75 g (3 oz) dried split peas

900 ml (1 1/2 pints) vegetable stock
or water

2 aubergines, diced

3 drumsticks, trimmed and cut
into 4 pieces

15 g (1/2 oz) coriander

salt and pepper

boiled rice, to serve

Serves 4

The Indian vegetable known as drumstick is rather like a bean. Choose drumsticks that are as fresh as possible – sometimes the outside can be dry and inedible. If the outsides are dry, scrape the pulp from inside and discard the dry shell. This Subji (vegetable curry) is ideal served with hard-boiled eggs or with chapati, puri or naan breads instead of rice.

1. Heat a large dry pan until hot, add the mustard seeds and toast until the seeds begin to pop. Add the garam masala, cassia bark, ground coriander, ground cumin, paprika and turmeric and toast, stirring occasionally, until the spices release their aromas.

2. Remove the spices from the pan and set aside. Add the onions and half the oil to the pan and cook gently to wilt and then caramelize the onions. Cover the pan and cook slowly for a further 10 minutes. Add the toasted spices, together with the garlic and split peas, and coat in oil.

3. Add the stock or water and bring to the boil. Continue to boil for 10 minutes, cover the pan and simmer for 10 further minutes.

4. In a separate pan, fry the aubergines and drumsticks in the remaining oil until golden brown and then add to the spiced sauce and cook gently for 25 minutes more. Season to taste with salt and pepper. Stir in the coriander leaves and serve with rice.

fruit & vegetable information: drumstick page 70; aubergine page 79

puréed yams with
venison sausages & salsa verde

750 g (1¹/₂ lb) yams

50 g (2 oz) butter

75 g (3 oz) Cheddar cheese, grated

150 ml (¹/₄ pint) crème fraîche

salt and pepper

Salsa verde

2 garlic cloves, crushed

4 tablespoons chopped parsley

1 tablespoon chopped chives

¹/₂ tablespoon chopped sage

25 g (1 oz) Parmesan cheese, grated

¹/₂ teaspoon chilli flakes

4 tablespoons olive oil

To serve

cooked venison sausages or thick slices of smoked ham

roasted tomatoes

olive oil, for drizzling

Serves 4

Yams and sweet potatoes are everyday food in Cuba where pork steaks are served with the mash. This is a more elegant version of this marriage of meat and yams and uses venison sausages or thick slices of good smoked ham. A quick and easy supper dish for summer or winter.

1. Peel the yams, cut into chunks and cook in boiling water for 30 minutes or until the yams are soft when tested with the tip of a knife. Drain well and roughly mash with the butter and Cheddar cheese.

2. Season the purée well with salt and pepper. Stir in the crème fraîche, remove from the heat, cover and set aside until the salsa verde is ready.

3. Put the garlic, parsley, chives and sage in a food processor or blender and process to a rough paste. Stir in the Parmesan and chilli flakes and then bind with the olive oil

4. Divide the puréed yam between 4 plates, add the sausages or smoked ham and top with the salsa verde. Serve with roasted tomatoes and a drizzle of olive oil.

fruit & vegetable information: yam page 60

marinated valentine
pork steaks with kiwi salsa

Valentine pork steaks are thick loin chops that have been cut through horizontally and opened out. This allows the steaks to cook more quickly and evenly. Add the kiwi salsa for a fresh edge and an impact of colour and flavour. Cook and assemble the salsa as close to serving as possible. The meat will be succulent and the salsa vibrant.

4 valentine pork steaks or loin steaks

1 tablespoon mixed peppercorns, roughly crushed

2 tablespoons honey

1 tablespoon lime juice

4 sage leaves

roasted tomatoes, to serve

salt

Kiwi salsa

1 red onion, finely chopped

1 small red pepper, deseeded and finely chopped

1 tablespoon chopped flat leaf parsley

2 kiwis

salt and pepper

Serves 4

1. Season the pork steaks with salt and then sprinkle the crushed peppercorns over them. Mix the honey with the lime juice. Put the pork steaks in a shallow dish and pour the honey and lime mixture over the pork. Chill in the refrigerator for 2 hours or overnight to marinate.

2. Mix the chopped red onion with the chopped red pepper and parsley, and season to taste with salt and pepper. Thinly peel the skin off the kiwis. Roughly chop the kiwis and mix the flesh and juice with the red onion mixture.

3. Preheat a griddle pan or grill. Top each steak with a sage leaf and cook the steaks for 3–4 minutes on each side or until the steaks are just cooked and still succulent.

4. Serve the pork steaks immediately with roasted tomatoes and top with the kiwi and red pepper salsa.

fruit & vegetable information: kiwi page 12

Duck à l'orange *is a French classic but here it has been simplified into duck portions served with a quick kumquat sauce that can be slowly simmered as the duck cooks in the oven to a wonderful crispiness.*

4 duck leg portions

1/2 teaspoon Chinese five-spice powder

300 ml (1/2 pint) orange or pink grapefruit juice

2 tablespoons clear honey

2 cloves

1 tablespoon Cointreau or brandy

10 kumquats, sliced

1 tablespoon chopped flat leaf parsley

salt and pepper

To serve

boiled potatoes

green vegetables

Serves 4

1. Place the duck legs on a rack standing inside a baking tin, season well with salt, pepper and Chinese five-spice powder and roast in a preheated oven at 220°C (425°F), Gas Mark 7 for 35 minutes.

2. Put the orange juice and honey in a saucepan with the cloves and Cointreau and bring to the boil. Boil for 2 minutes, reduce the heat and add the kumquat slices. Simmer for 10 minutes.

3. Remove the duck from the oven and add to the pan with the kumquat sauce. Simmer gently together for 10 minutes.

4. Add the chopped parsley to the sauce, thickly slice the duck and serve piping hot with boiled potatoes and green vegetables.

fruit & vegetable information: kumquat page 32

roasted duck legs
with kumquat & honey sauce

sweet sour chicken
with lychees & ginger

2 onions, roughly chopped

1 garlic clove, crushed

5 cm (2 in) piece of fresh
root ginger, grated

1 tablespoon vegetable oil

500 g (1 lb) skinless chicken breast

50 g (2 oz) plain flour

2 eggs, beaten

300 ml (½ pint) cold water

vegetable oil, for deep-frying

2 carrots, peeled and cut into
julienne strips

25 g (1 oz) caster sugar

1 tablespoon tomato purée

150 ml (¼ pint) pineapple juice

1 tablespoon cornflour

400 g (13 oz) can lychees in syrup

2 tablespoons white wine
or rice vinegar

salt and pepper

Serves 4

This is light and delicious; fry the meat just before serving and toss in the sauce as it goes to the table. This way the chicken pieces keep their crisp coating. The lychees add a crisp texture and a sweet flavour. Use canned lychees and add the syrup to the sauce.

1. Fry the onions gently in a saucepan with the garlic, ginger and oil for 1 minute. Cut the chicken into small cubes and dust with plain flour.

2. Mix the remaining plain flour with salt and pepper, the beaten eggs and water. Beat until a smooth batter forms and leave to stand for 15 minutes.

3. Heat the oil in a deep saucepan until a cube of bread added to the hot oil browns in 3 minutes. Dip the chicken pieces into the batter and then lower into the hot oil. Deep-fry 6–8 pieces of chicken at a time for 3–4 minutes or until the batter is golden brown and the chicken cooked through. Remove from the oil with a slotted spoon and drain on kitchen paper. Keep warm while cooking the remainder of the chicken.

4. Add the strips of carrot and the sugar to the onions and stir together. Add the tomato purée and the pineapple juice and slowly bring to the boil. Mix the cornflour with a little of the lychee syrup, reserving the remaining syrup and lychees, until the cornflour becomes a smooth runny paste.

5. Add the lychee syrup to the saucepan containing the sauce and mix together. Add the cornflour paste and, stirring constantly, bring slowly to the boil. Reduce the heat and simmer for a further 5–6 minutes or until the sauce has thickened.

6. Add the lychees and the vinegar to the sauce and simmer for a further 1 minute. Pour the sauce over the fried chicken pieces and serve immediately.

fruit & vegetable information: lychees page 35

roasted pork
with papaya & green chilli salsa

Papaya has a wonderful fresh flavour that pairs well with meat and other fruits. It also has a wonderful tenderizing action on meat and makes a great marinade for pork, chicken and lamb. One of the ingredients that brings the best flavour out of papaya is lime. Here it binds the papaya salsa, highlighting the flavours and keeping the colours of the salsa vibrant.

2 kg (4 lb) leg or loin of pork

2 papayas, peeled, deseeded and roughly chopped

juice and finely grated rind of 2 limes

400 g (13 oz) can cannellini beans, drained

2 tablespoons chopped coriander

2 tomatoes, chopped

1 small green chilli, deseeded and chopped

8–10 sage leaves

salt and pepper

Serves 6

1. Season the pork all over with salt and pepper. Purée half the papaya flesh in a food processor or blender, or pass it through a fine sieve. Mix the papaya purée with half the lime juice and smear it all over the leg of pork. Leave to marinate for 2 hours or overnight.

2. Put the pork on a rack in a baking tin and roast in a preheated oven at 190°C (375°F), Gas Mark 5 for 30 minutes per 500 g (1 lb) or until the pork is tender and cooked right through.

3. Meanwhile, mix the remaining chopped papaya with the remaining lime juice and the grated lime rind. Season to taste with salt and pepper and stir in the cannellini beans, the coriander, tomatoes and the chopped green chilli. Mix well and chill until ready to serve.

4. Arrange the sage leaves on top of the pork 30 minutes before the end of cooking and cook until crisp. Serve the pork thickly sliced with the salsa and juices.

fruit & vegetable information: papaya page 17; chillies page 57

moroccan duck
with pomegranate & walnut sauce

Pomegranate juice is very refreshing and slightly sweet and sour – these characteristics are ideal with fatty meats like lamb and duck. In North Africa these large fruits, packed with seeds, are used in meat dishes and in particular with duck, walnuts or almonds. This is a very simple version of one of the Middle Eastern classics – Faisanjan. Serve with plain rice and a side dish of yogurt. You may find cans or bottles of pomegranate juice – this can be substituted, but the fresh fruit yields the best juice.

2 tablespoons olive oil

2 onions, chopped

1 teaspoon turmeric

250 g (8 oz) walnut pieces

450 ml (³/₄ pint) water, chicken or vegetable stock

4 duck portions

8 tablespoons lemon juice

2 tablespoons caster sugar

4 pomegranates, plus extra to garnish

salt and pepper

boiled rice, to serve

Serves 4

1. Heat the oil in a large casserole and gently fry the chopped onions until softened and beginning to brown. Add the turmeric, stir to mix and fry gently for 1 minute.

2. Grind the walnut pieces into a fine powder using a food processor, blender, or a pestle and mortar and add to the onions with the water or stock. Bring to a gentle simmer and cook for a further 20 minutes.

3. Heat a dry frying pan and fry the duck portions on all sides until the skin is crisp and golden brown. Remove the duck from the pan, draining away the excess fat, and add to the walnut sauce. Cover the pan and simmer gently for 1 hour.

4. Add the lemon juice, sugar, and salt and pepper to the pan and mix well. Take each pomegranate in turn and gently crush and roll the fruit in the hand to release each of the pips and burst the juice sacks. This will take about 5 minutes. When the fruit feels soft, pierce the skin and the juice will pour out. Add this juice to the pan, cover with a lid and simmer for a further 30 minutes. Serve with a few extra pomegranate seeds sprinkled over the duck and with plain boiled rice.

fruit & vegetable information: pomegranate page 47

3 sweet white onions, sliced

2 tablespoons vegetable oil

5 cm (2 in) piece of fresh root ginger, finely chopped

1 cinnamon stick

10 saffron threads

1 teaspoon ground cumin

pinch of cayenne pepper

750 g (1½ lb) shoulder of lamb, cubed

2 carrots, peeled and cut into 5 cm (2 in) pieces

600 ml (1 pint) chicken or vegetable stock, or water

2 tablespoons honey

500 g (1 lb) dates

4 tablespoons lemon juice

2 tablespoons toasted almonds

2 tablespoons sour cherries

salt and pepper

To serve

250 g (8 oz) cooked couscous

preserved lemons (optional)

chopped mint

Serves 4

lamb & sour cherry tagine

This fragrant Moroccan tagine of lamb cooks slowly in a rich gravy until the meat is tender and succulent. Dates, almonds and sour cherries are added towards the end of cooking to preserve their individual flavours.

1. Briefly fry the onions in the oil until wilted. Add the ginger, cinnamon stick, saffron, cumin and cayenne pepper and fry for 1 further minute. Remove the onions from the pan and reserve.

2. Add some of the lamb to the hot pan and quickly cook on all sides to brown. Remove from the pan and set aside. Brown the remaining meat in batches to keep the pan hot and prevent the meat from braising in its own juices.

3. Return the onions and lamb to the pan and add the carrots, and enough stock or water to cover the meat. Bring to the boil, cover and simmer slowly for 2 hours. When the meat is tender, remove it from the sauce and set aside. Increase the heat and boil until the sauce is reduced and thick. Return the meat to the pan.

4. Add the honey, dates and lemon juice and simmer uncovered for 10 minutes or until the dates are tender and the sauce is reduced and thick. Season to taste with salt and pepper. Add the toasted almonds and sour cherries and simmer for a further 5 minutes.

5. Serve the tagine on a bed of hot couscous, preserved lemons, if using, and chopped mint.

fruit & vegetable information: dates page 44

A light and refreshing sorbet made from this papaya-like fruit. If you do not have a Jamaican or West Indian market or supplier close to your shopping area, substitute the babacos with ripe papayas. A squeeze of lime added at the last minute adds an extra edge. Serve in small glass jars or shot glasses at drinks or summer parties. Fabulous with little coconut biscuits.

125 g (4 oz) granulated sugar

150 ml (¼ pint) cold water

500 g (1 lb) babacos or ripe papaya

juice and grated rind of 2 limes

lime wedges, to decorate

Serves 4

1. Put the granulated sugar in a saucepan with the water and heat gently to dissolve the sugar. Increase the heat, bring to the boil and stop stirring. Boil for 5 minutes. Remove from the heat and allow to cool.

2. Peel the babacos or papaya and dice the flesh. Reserve 2 tablespoons of the diced flesh and put the remainder in a food processor or blender with the cooled sugar syrup and process until smooth.

3. Add the lime juice and grated rind to the babacos purée and pour into a shallow metal container. Freeze for 3 hours.

4. Remove from the freezer and beat with a fork to break up the ice crystals. Stir in the reserved diced babacos flesh, return to the freezer and freeze until solid.

5. Remove from the freezer 10 minutes before serving and scoop into small glasses. Serve topped with a lime wedge.

fruit & vegetable information: babacos page 18; papaya page 17

babacos
& lime sorbet

fresh custard apple
& mango tartlets

Custard apples are, as their name suggests, full of the flavour of the best custard that you will ever taste – light, smooth and full of vanilla. That is the reason for adding them to a freshly baked pastry shell and topping them with sweet and fragrant mango slices. Fresh fruit at its best.

1. Roll out the pastry and line six 12.5 cm (5 in) tartlet tins. Line with greaseproof paper and baking beans and bake blind in a preheated oven at 200°C (400°F), Gas Mark 6 for 10 minutes. Remove the grease-proof paper and beans and return to the oven for 5 minutes.

2. Spread the conserve over the base of the warm pastry shells. Cut the custard apples in half, scoop out the flesh and put in a bowl. Remove and discard the large pips and beat the custard apple flesh with the honey until smooth and creamy.

500 g (1 lb) sweet shortcrust pastry

6 tablespoons apricot conserve

3. Scrape the seeds out of the vanilla pod, add them to the custard apple flesh together with the cream and divide between the pastry shells.

3 custard apples

1 tablespoon clear honey

4. Cut the mango flesh off the stone, peel away the skin and slice the flesh. Arrange the slices on top of the custard apple cream. Dust heavily with icing sugar and serve topped with mint leaves.

1 vanilla pod, split

2 tablespoons double cream

1 small mango

icing sugar, for dusting

mint leaves, to decorate

Serves 6

fruit & vegetable information: custard apple page 14; mango page 36

rambutan & **peach** ice cream

Rambutans, lychees and longans are all similar in flavour and have a similar textured flesh held around a central stone. If you find there are plenty on sale at a good price, make this fresh and fragrant ice cream. Otherwise use canned fruit and serve with a simple fruit salad or with biscuits or wafers.

1. Put the rambutans, peaches and ginger in a food processor or blender and process to a coarse purée.

2. Put the peach syrup in a measuring jug and make up to 600 ml (1 pint) with water. Put the syrup into a saucepan with the sugar and heat gently until the sugar has dissolved. Remove from the heat and leave to cool. When cold stir the syrup into the fruit purée with the lime juice and cream. Pour the mixture into a large baking tray and freeze.

3. When the mixture has begun to freeze, mix with a fork to break up the big crystals. Refreeze. Whisk the egg white until standing in peaks and stir into the half-frozen ice cream and freeze again. Serve scooped into a dish with fresh or tinned rambutans or lychees.

500 g (1 lb) rambutans, peeled and stoned

200 g (7 oz) can peaches in natural syrup, drained and syrup reserved

1 tablespoon finely grated fresh root ginger

175 g (6 oz) caster sugar

125 ml (4 fl oz) lime juice

300 ml (½ pint) double cream

1 egg white

rambutans or lychees, to serve

Serves 4

baked fig
& frangipani tart

*Figs and almonds are a popular Mediterranean mixture.
Here slices of fresh fig lie on top of rolled marzipan and are
quickly cooked in a hot oven to allow the pastry base to puff
and cook through, while warming the marzipan and figs.*

1. Roll out the pastry, cut six 12 cm (5 in) rounds and
place on a damp baking tray.

2. Roll out the marzipan and cut into 10 cm (4 in)
rounds. Place directly on top of the puff pastry rounds.

500 g (1 lb) puff pastry

3. Slice the figs and arrange on top of the marzipan.
Cook in the centre of a preheated oven at
220°C (425°F), Gas Mark 7 for 8 minutes.

250 g (8 oz) marzipan

6 firm, but ripe figs

4. Melt the butter and the sugar together and drizzle
over the tartlets. Return to the oven for a further
5 minutes. Serve warm, dusted with icing sugar,
accompanied by crème fraîche.

25 g (1 oz) butter

2 tablespoons caster sugar

icing sugar, for dusting

crème fraîche, to serve

Serves 6

caramelized pineapple
with burnt cointreau syrup

2 queen pineapples

1 orange

25 g (1 oz) butter

1 vanilla pod

2 tablespoons caster sugar

1 tablespoon Cointreau

75 g (3 oz) flaked almonds, toasted

3 tablespoons orange juice

thick Greek yogurt or single cream, to serve

Serves 4

The strong texture of the pineapple makes this dessert possible. It caramelizes beautifully in the pan and is then dressed with a burnt Cointreau syrup. Serve still lingering with warmth. If small queen pineapples are not available, use another super-sweet variety.

1. Cut the leaves off the pineapples and then cut away the skin. Slice the pineapples thickly and then cut each slice into chunks.

2. Cut the peel and the pith off the orange and then divide the flesh into segments and mix with the pineapple chunks.

3. Heat the butter in a wok or large frying pan until melted and beginning to bubble. Add the pineapple and orange together and cook over a high heat for 1–2 minutes or until beginning to brown.

4. Cut the vanilla pod in half, scrape out the seeds and mix them with the caster sugar. Add the vanilla caster sugar and Cointreau to the wok and quickly stir-fry until the pieces of fruit are caramelized.

5. Add the toasted almonds and orange juice and stir-fry for 2 minutes or until the juices become syrupy. Serve immediately while the fruit is still warm, accompanied with thick Greek yogurt or single cream.

fruit & vegetable information: queen pineapple page 13

coconut ice cream
with palm fruit seeds

These jelly-like palm fruit seeds are often found stirred into coconut and fruit ice cream in China or Thailand. They are candied and cooked in syrup and then added to desserts for their interesting texture. They are at their best in and on top of ice cream. Look for them in Asian stores in glass jars. Keep chilled in the refrigerator.

400 ml (14 fl oz) can coconut milk

300 ml (1/2 pint) double cream

250 ml (8 fl oz) milk

1 vanilla pod

6 egg yolks

175 g (6 oz) caster sugar

50 g (2 oz) desiccated or grated fresh coconut

4 tablespoons candied palm fruit seeds

Serves 6

1. Put the coconut milk, cream and milk in a saucepan with the vanilla pod and slowly bring to the boil. Remove from the heat and leave to cool. Slit the vanilla pod in half along its length and scrape out the tiny seeds with the tip of a knife. Add the seeds to the coconut mixture.

2. Whisk the egg yolks and sugar in a large bowl and then gradually whisk the warm coconut milk and desiccated or fresh coconut into the eggs. Pour this mixture into a saucepan and slowly heat, while stirring constantly, for 5–10 minutes or until the mixture thickens slightly to a custard and the eggs have cooked. Be careful to not overcook or the eggs will scramble.

3. Pour the mixture into a metal container and, when cold, place in the freezer. When the mixture has started to freeze, whisk in a blender or with a fork to break up the big ice crystals. Return to the freezer and freeze until solid.

4. Serve scooped into a bowl with palm fruit seeds on top.

passion fruit
& lime posset

A very sharp and refreshing dessert which cuts the richness of the cream. The basic recipe dates back to Elizabethan England and has been brought up to date with the addition of passion fruit. The cream mixture is poured into glasses while still runny and will set as it chills.

450 ml (³/₄ pint) double or whipping cream

50 g (2 oz) caster sugar

juice and finely grated rind of 2 limes

2 tablespoons sweet wine or sherry

5 passion fruits

icing sugar, for dusting (optional)

amaretti or almond biscuits, to serve (optional)

Serves 4

1. Put the cream in a heavy-based saucepan with the sugar and slowly heat until the sugar has dissolved. Increase the heat and boil for 5 minutes, taking care not to burn the bottom of the cream.

2. Remove from the heat and beat with an electric mixer for 2 minutes. Add the lime juice and grated rind together with the sweet wine and carry on beating for 2 minutes. Chill for 1 hour or until beginning to set.

3. Cut 4 passion fruits in half and scoop out the seeds and flesh with a teaspoon. Break up the flesh with the spoon and then roughly fold it into the setting cream.

4. Divide the mixture between 4 small glass dishes. Chill for 2 hours or overnight. Just before serving, cut the remaining passion fruit in half and scoop out the seeds and drizzle over the top of the possets. Dust heavily with icing sugar and serve with amaretti or almond biscuits, if liked.

fruit & vegetable information: passion fruit page 41

persimmon
& star anise jelly

Fruit jellies can be just as sophisticated as any tart or cream-laced dessert. It is how they are made and what is put inside them that elevates them from nursery food. Experiment with fresh exotic fruits like lychees, mango, passion fruits and guavas. Dice the fruit quite small and, to prevent all the pieces from settling to the bottom of the jelly, leave the jelly to reach a point when it just begins to set and then stir in the fruit.

600 ml (1 pint) orange or mango juice

1 star anise

75 g (3 oz) caster sugar

15 g (1/2 oz) gelatine

2 persimmons

75 g (3 oz) blueberries

To serve

physalis and thick slices of persimmon

single cream (optional)

Serves 6

1. Measure out 6 tablespoons of the orange or mango juice and set aside. Add the star anise to the remaining juice and the sugar and heat gently for 2–3 minutes, stirring frequently, until the sugar has dissolved. Remove from the heat and allow to stand until cold. Remove and discard the star anise.

2. Put the reserved orange or mango juice and the gelatine in a small bowl over a pan of gently simmering water and leave to warm until the gelatine has dissolved.

3. Remove the gelatine from the heat, leave to cool for 5 minutes and then stir it into the orange juice. Pour the mixture into a 600 ml (1 pint) loaf tin or jelly mould or into 6 individual jelly moulds. Chill in the refrigerator for 20 minutes.

4. Cut the tops off the persimmons, peel back the skin and cut the flesh into small dice. Mix the persimmons with the blueberries and stir into the orange or mango jelly which will have begun to set. Return to the refrigerator and leave for 4 hours or overnight to set firmly.

5. Dip the tin, mould or moulds into warm water to loosen the jelly, then turn out on to a plate. Serve topped with physalis and slices of persimmon and single cream, if liked.

fruit & vegetable information: mango page 36; persimmon page 27; physalis page 45

baked tamarillo
tarts

400 g (13 oz) sweetcrust pastry

50 g (2 oz) caster sugar

1 vanilla pod, halved

150 ml (¼ pint) orange juice

3 tamarillos

125 g (4 oz) ground almonds

125 g (4 oz) caster sugar

50 g (2 oz) butter

3 medium eggs, beaten

5 tablespoons plum jam

icing sugar, for dusting

thick cream or crème fraîche, to serve

Serves 6

The tamarillo is one of those fruits that no one seems to know what to do with. Here they are gently poached in a sugar syrup and added to a bakewell tart. Serve with a thick dusting of icing sugar and thick cream or crème fraîche.

1. Roll out the pastry and use it to line a 20 cm (8 in) loose-bottomed flan tin or 4 individual 10 cm (4 in) loose-bottomed tart tins. Fill with greaseproof paper and baking beans and bake blind in a preheated oven at 200°C (400°F), Gas Mark 6 for 10 minutes. Remove the paper and beans and return to the oven for a further 5 minutes, leaving the oven on when you remove the pastry case.

2. Put half the sugar in a small saucepan with the vanilla pod and orange juice and heat gently to dissolve the sugar. Add the tamarillos to the orange juice and gently poach for 5 minutes. Remove from the heat.

3. Cream the butter with the remaining sugar until soft and fluffy and gradually add the beaten eggs. Beat well and then add the ground almonds. Mix well. Spread the plum jam over the bottom of the pastry and then spoon the cake mixture over the top.

4. Remove the tamarillos from the juice. Peel away and discard the skin and then cut in half and place on the top of the cake mixture. Bake in the centre of the oven for 10–12 minutes for individual tarts or 20 minutes for a large one or until the sponge has risen and is firm to the touch.

5. Boil the orange syrup until reduced and thickened and brush over the tamarillos. Leave to cool. Dust with icing sugar and serve with thick cream or crème fraîche.

fruit & vegetable information: tamarillo page 26

ugli, mint &
lemon grass sorbet

A citrus sorbet with a hint of sweetness and sharpness from the unusual ugli fruit and the zestiness of lemon grass. Ideal between courses or as a dessert.

125 g (4 oz) granulated sugar

300 ml (½ pint) cold water

1 lemon grass stalk, finely chopped

2 ugli fruits

2 tablespoons chopped mint

8 tablespoons Cointreau

rolled wafer biscuits, to serve

Serves 6

1. Put the sugar in a pan with the water and heat gently to dissolve the sugar. Increase the heat and bring the syrup to the boil. Boil for 2 minutes without stirring.

2. Add the chopped lemon grass to the syrup, simmer for a further 10 minutes, remove from the heat and leave to cool. When the syrup is cold, strain to remove the lemon grass.

3. Peel the ugli fruit and remove all the white pith. Put the flesh in a food processor or blender and process briefly to a rough purée. Add the purée to the cold syrup and mix well. Add the chopped mint and pour into a shallow metal container. Freeze for 3 hours.

4. Remove from the freezer and mix with a fork to break up the ice crystals. Return to the freezer and freeze until firm.

5. Remove from the freezer 30 minutes before serving and leave in the refrigerator to soften. Scoop into small dishes, pour the Cointreau over the scoops of sorbet and serve immediately with rolled wafers.

fruit & vegetable information: ugli fruit page 22

toffee
& sesame bananas

6 ripe bananas

1 egg, lightly beaten

4 tablespoons sesame seeds

5 tablespoons dried breadcrumbs

oil, for deep-frying

**crème fraîche or thick cream,
to serve**

Toffee sauce

25 g (1 oz) butter

1 tablespoon rum

150 g (5 oz) dark brown sugar

50 ml (2 fl oz) water

200 ml (7 fl oz) coconut milk

150 ml (¼ pint) double cream

Serves 4

Pisang goreng, *as it is known, is a hawkers food in South-east Asia and is eaten at all times of the day. This version is a little more sophisticated and makes a fabulous dessert to serve at a more formal suppertime. Any type of bananas can be used but the little apple bananas are excellent with their firm texture and distinctive flavour.*

1. Cut the bananas in half, dip in the beaten egg and then into the sesame seeds and breadcrumbs.

2. Heat the oil in a large saucepan until a cube of bread added to the oil browns in 3 minutes. Fry the bananas for 1–2 minutes or until golden brown. Drain on kitchen paper and keep warm.

3. Melt the butter in a pan and then add the rum and sugar with the water and heat gently until the sugar has dissolved. Stir the coconut milk and cream into the syrup and increase the heat. Bring to the boil, reduce the heat and simmer gently for 5 minutes. Remove from the heat and serve with the hot bananas and crème fraîche or thick cream.

physalis
conserve

A light and delicious conserve, spread on fruit breads, scones and Victoria sandwiches. Physalis (Cape gooseberry) jam is especially enjoyed in Cape Town. It was here that my grandmother would make this conserve when the local fruits were in abundance in late February. Obviously that's fine when you are living in the country of origin, but sometimes you may see physalis at a greatly reduced price – and there are only so many one can use in a fruit salad. It's then that this recipe comes into its own.

500 g (1 lb) physalis

500 g (1 lb) jam sugar

7 cm (3 in) piece of fresh root ginger, finely chopped

1 small lemon, halved

3 tablespoons water

Makes 1 kg (2 lb)

1. Remove the paper-like petals from the fruit and put all the physalis berries in a colander and wash.

2. Put the preserving sugar in a large heavy-based pan with the washed berries, chopped ginger and the halved lemon. Add the water and heat gently, stirring occasionally.

3. Cook gently for 10 minutes, stirring occasionally to dissolve the sugar. Increase the heat and bring the jam to the boil. When a full rolling boil is achieved, boil for a further 8 minutes at 105°C (220°F) on a jam thermometer.

4. To test the set of the jam, pour a little of the hot mixture on to a saucer and leave to cool. If setting point has been reached, the surface will wrinkle when pushed with a finger.

5. Remove from the heat, skim off any scum and remove and discard the lemon shells. Leave to stand for 15 minutes to allow the fruit to settle. Stir once again and pour into clean, warmed jars. Cover and label. Serve with fruit or plain bread or with toast, croissants or rolls.

fruit & vegetable information: physalis page 45

mango
chutney

Geeta Samtani has taught me the most about chutney and in particular mango chutney. She has her own business making the finest Indian chutneys under her own name, Geeta's. Tamarind, mango, pineapple and lime are particular favourites, she has inspired this recipe. If I'm ever in a market and see a box full of ripe mangoes going for a song, it's mango ice cream and spiced mango chutney all round.

1 kg (2 lb) fresh mangoes

3 whole cloves

1 teaspoon onion seeds

pinch of crushed dried chillies

1/2 teaspoon black peppercorns

500 g (1 lb) preserving or jam sugar

2 garlic cloves, crushed

4 tablespoons white wine vinegar

1/2 teaspoon salt

Makes 1 kg (2 lb)

1. Cut the mangoes in half, down either side of the stone. Peel away the skin and cut the mango flesh into thick strips.

2. Put the mango pieces, the spices, the sugar and the crushed garlic into a large heavy-based saucepan and heat gently, stirring occasionally, until the sugar has dissolved.

3. Increase the heat and bring the mango mixture to the boil. When at a full rolling boil (see page 167), boil for a further 5 minutes.

4. Remove from the heat and allow to cool slightly. Stir in the vinegar and the salt and mix well. Leave to stand for a further 5 minutes and then pour into clean, warmed jars. Cover and label.

guava, apple
& banana smoothie

Smoothies have been all the rage for the past couple of years – they are full of goodness and an ideal way to kick off the day or to quickly substitute lunch, when all you have time for is food on the run.

2 ripe guavas

1 apple, peeled, cored and roughly chopped

2 bananas, thickly sliced

125 g (4 oz) raspberries or strawberries

200 ml (7 fl oz) natural yogurt

150 ml (¼ pint) cold water

ice cubes

Serves 4

1. Thinly peel the guavas, cut in half and remove the seeds from the centre. Roughly chop the flesh and place in a food processor or blender with the chopped apple and banana. Process until smooth.

2. Add the raspberries or strawberries together with the yogurt and water. Process again until smooth. Pour over ice cubes and drink immediately.

fruit & vegetable information: guava page 46; apple banana page 38

watermelon & passion fruit
breakfast juice

This is a bright and reviving combo juice to take first thing in the morning. The subtle mix of watermelon and passion fruit puts a spring in your step. Use honeydew or cantaloupe melon instead of watermelon if you prefer, with strawberries or raspberries for a change. Include the watermelon seeds – they are full of essential minerals.

500 g (1 lb) watermelon flesh

150 ml (¼ pint) water

4 passion fruits

2 tablespoons lime juice

1 tablespoon icing sugar

To serve

ice cubes

lime or watermelon wedges

Serves 4

1. Roughly cut up the watermelon flesh and put in a food processor or blender with the water. Process well until perfectly smooth and slushy.

2. Cut the passion fruits in half and scoop out the seeds. Mix with the puréed watermelon juice, the lime juice and icing sugar. Blend together.

3. Pour the juice into tumblers of ice and serve with wedges of lime or thick wedges of watermelon.

fruit & vegetable information: watermelon page 19; passion fruit page 41

sapodilla &
cardamom milkshake

Otherwise known as Chico milkshakes, these are a great favourite of Indian children – especially my friend Daxxa's two. When ripe, these plum-shaped fruits have a delicious custard-like flavour that blends to make a rich milkshake. All too often, fruits turn ripe at the same time – so making a long cool drink like this is an ideal way to use them up. If a whole bargain box is found on sale at a greatly reduced price, then it's chico juice for everyone.

4–6 sapodillas

2 green cardamom pods

1. Cut the sapodillas in half and scoop out the flesh. Discard the pips and put the flesh in a food processor or blender. Process until smooth.

600 ml (1 pint) milk

2 teaspoons lemon juice

2. Crush the cardamom pods with a rolling pin or the back of a heavy knife and remove the seeds. Add the seeds to the food processor or blender together with the milk and lemon juice.

To serve

crushed ice

3. Blend the mixture well until smooth and frothy. Pour the drink over tumblers of ice. Sprinkle with freshly grated nutmeg and serve immediately.

grated nutmeg

Serves 2

fruit & vegetable information: sapodilla page 37

nimbu
pani

4 limes

2 kaffir lime leaves

4 tablespoons caster sugar

600 ml (1 pint) boiling water

pinch of salt

To serve

ice cubes

pared lime rind

Serves 4

This is a great thirst quencher from the days of India's Raj – my aunt Feh Hume, as she was then, remembers this refreshing drink served at all the gatherings and club house verandahs, as they sipped and listened to the sound of the bagpipes of the Rajaputana rifles. That was a long time ago, back in the 1920s, but nimbu pani *still lives on in those fragrant foothills of pine cones and betel nuts. The lime leaves are a new addition, and of course are not Indian, but add an extra citrus twist.*

1. Cut the limes in half, squeeze the juice and reserve.

2. Put the lime shells, lime leaves and the caster sugar into a jug and pour over the boiling water. Leave to stand for 15 minutes. No longer or the juice will become bitter.

3. Add the pinch of salt to the liquid in the jug and stir together.

4. Strain the infusion on to the fresh lime juice and add ice. Set aside to cool. When ready to serve, pour over tall tumblers of ice and serve with a twizzle of lime rind.

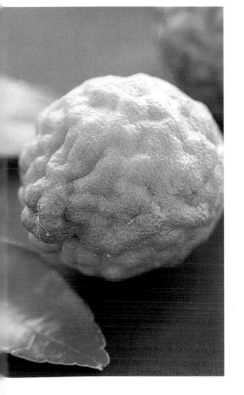

index

Author's thanks and acknowledgments:

This book would not have been possible without the help and invaluable advise of Daxxa Amin,
Adrian Heath-Saunders, Jean Stoddart, Peter Reid, Robin Revel-Johnson, Geeta Samtani,
Bhavin's in Tooting, Talad Thai in Putney, Hyams & Cockerton in Wandsworth, Jo Younger,
Emma Marsden, Vicky Walters, Ian Wallace, Sarah Ford & Gnos Garlic Company in Oregon.